MOORESTOWN LIBRARY
MOORESTOWN. N. J. 08057

Moorestown Library

3 2030 00090 4697
NJML Oversized 746.44q E
c1976.
Edmonds, Mary Jaene.
Geometric designs in needlepoin

P9-CDT-206

OVERSIZED   152393
746.44q
Edm   Edmonds, Mary Jaene.
            Geometric designs in
         needlepoint

circ : 4
LAD 4/2006

Moorestown Library
Moorestown, New Jersey
08057

GEOMETRIC DESIGNS IN NEEDLEPOINT

GEOMETRIC DESIGNS IN NEEDLEPOINT

Mary Jaene Edmonds

VNR

VAN NOSTRAND REINHOLD COMPANY
New York Cincinnati Toronto London Melbourne

To Jim

Acknowledgments

I would like to thank some of the people who are responsible for the publication of this book. First, my dear husband, for more reasons than I have space to list; to my cardiologist, Dr. H. R. Casdorph, M.D. who allowed me to needlepoint when he might have thought it unwise; to Estelle Horowitz, who recognized something special in my work and to whom I am especially indebted; to Lee Pierce, a dear friend, who mounted the needlepoint so beautifully and who gave me lots of encouragement; and to Mr. Yasushi Sakimoto who spent hours helping me perfect and assemble the Victorian picture frame.

746.44g
Edm

Library of Congress Catalog Card Number 75-3860
ISBN 0-442-22238-6 (cloth)

All rights reserved. No part of this work
may be reproduced or used in any form or by any
means—graphic, electronic, or mechanical, including photocopying, recording, taping, or information storage and retrieval systems—without permission of the publisher.
Printed in Germany by Mohn-Bertelsmann Corporation.
Designed by Loudan Enterprises.
Photographs by Malcolm Varon, except those on pages 121–124, which are by F. J. Thomas.

Published in 1976 by Van Nostrand Reinhold Company
A Division of Litton Educational Publishing, Inc.
450 West 33rd Street
New York, NY 10001, U.S.A.

Van Nostrand Reinhold Limited
1410 Birchmount Road
Scarborough, Ontario M1P 2E7, Canada

Van Nostrand Reinhold Australia Pty. Ltd.
17 Queen Street
Mitcham, Victoria 3132, Australia

Van Nostrand Reinhold Company Ltd.
Molly Millars Lane
Wokingham, Berkshire, England

16 15 14 13 12 11 10 9 8 7 6 5 4 3 2 1

Library of Congress Cataloging in Publication Data

Edmonds, Mary Jaene.
    Geometric designs in needlepoint.

    Bibliography: p. 129.
    Includes index.
    1. Canvas embroidery—Patterns. I. Title.
TT778.C3E35   746.4'4   75-3860
ISBN 0-442-22238-6

CONTENTS

152393

PREFACE

It began as a love affair with stitches, all kinds of needle-point stitches. And it was a long time in coming. Being the daughter of a true Southern Belle, I put in my share of hours doing lady-like needlework as a child. I can still recall spending my afternoons embroidering a golden colored cotton pillow with a black outline stitch around a blue dotted little girl. Miss Muffet, I think it was. I don't think I did a very good job of it, but my mother was satisfied enough to have it sewn into a small square pillow.

My father was an artist turned sign painter, so it was inevitable tht I should be able to draw, paint, sculpt, design jewelry, and finally end up as a fashion designer of sorts. All of the necessary skills became my repertoire: pattern drafting, draping, tailoring, millinery, etc. I sewed everything and enjoyed it.

But needlework, especially needlepoint, escaped me until in 1968. That was the year I had a near fatal heart attack which indeed changed my life. A dear friend and I had been shopping just before that January day, and impulsively she decided that we would do four chair seats for her dining room in needlepoint. The designs were already sewn on the canvases and, frankly, I had never seen such dreadful flowers. Besides, the fun part of doing *those* was already finished. We were to do only the background. The salesgirl knew absolutely nothing about what stitch we were to use. The canvas was penelope (I know now) and had lots of holes in it that apparently we were *not* to use. Somehow, we gathered enough information from the other customers and began. We used the half cross-stitch, and when I finally completed mine it was distorted beyond belief. I thought I'd done something terribly wrong, and ignorance did not satisfy me. The library contained some answers to my questions on this ancient art, and I set about determinedly to find them.

After my heart attack, the long hours in bed gave me the time for research. The necessary books, canvas, and yarns were purchased by my husband from hasty pleas written on hospital menus. He's a very sweet and patient man, so each day became a new and exciting one for me. One day he arrived with the *Sylvia Sidney Needlepoint Book* and I was a gonner. It's still one of my favorite books, and I'm glad I now have this opportunity to thank Sylvia Sidney for giving me such pleasure. Suddenly it was all there—I knew what canvas was all about, and how the basketweave stitch (diagonal tent stitch) would help keep my work straight, and that there was a treasure of all those other marvelous stitches waiting for me to learn about.

Since that time I have become an avid needlepointer, although I still consider myself a newcomer to the craft. It was such an exciting discovery for me that my time was consumed in reading and experimenting with my new-found knowledge. And as I became able to travel again, my husband and I would wander in strange European cities to find a particular shop just for the pleasure of seeing what yarns and books were available there.

I suppose it was at this point that I began to stray from the traditional concepts of what *should* be done to what *could* be done on canvas. I experimented with every stitch and every yarn I could find, seeming to prefer monochromatic color schemes that emphasized texture. Needlepoint is a geometric art form since the stitches cover a predictable number of canvas threads and fit together in a precise mathematical order. So, in addition to texture, I stressed geometric quality in my work.

This book, then, is about two basic forms of geometric needlepoint: repeat patterns and one-statement designs, which I call center motifs. The complete design in a repeat pattern is smaller than the finished work will be and in general uses only one or two stitches. It must be repeated rhythmically until the proper number of stitches have been made to complete the project. The one-statement pattern develops from a center motif and offers a wide field for variation in texture and contrast through the use of many different stitches. You will find both types of patterns among the 20 designs which I have created for this book, and you can create endless variations from them for yourself.

I. BASIC INFORMATION

The purpose of this book is to give you the pleasure of trying another form, another direction, in needlepoint design. The stitches are certainly not new, but their arrangement is. I hope you are already familiar with the various kinds of canvas and know how to work step by step to create the basic stitches. There are several excellent books in the Bibliography which can provide you with such introductory information, if you are a beginner. It is, however, my desire to give you the basic information needed to start right *now* to work on these geometric designs and to have you use them over and over again by experimenting with color, texture, and size. Each design has complete instructions, yarn color information, and a color photograph of the finished work so you can see how it will look.

Then, by varying the size of your canvas for instance, you can change the size of the design. If it is a center motif, you can make it bolder with larger canvas and larger yarn or as small and subtle as you choose by using smaller canvas, thinner yarns, and delicate colors. The possibilities are endless, as you shall see.

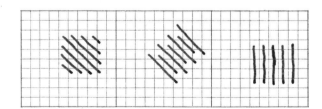

The Charts

Just a word or two about the variety of uses for these charts. I have made them into pillows, upholstery fabric, cushions, handbags, glasses cases, and photograph frames to show you that they can be most versatile and interchangeable. The small repeat patterns lend themselves to many, many uses. The center designs could be made up in squares and arranged with squares of solid color to become a handsome rug. Again, you must choose the design that is practical for your purpose.

Think of your needlepoint in terms of total design. If you are making a pillow, how shall it be finished? Do you plan to have a corded knife edge of contrasting color, perhaps? Will it look best boxed? Maybe you'd like some tassels on each corner to incorporate the many yarns you have used. All of these details must be considered as part of the complete design.

A knife-edged finishing creates a plain pillow; the top of the pillow and the bottom meet at the edge—no fancy stuff involved—as with the cutting edge of a knife. A welt, or cord, usually commercially made and often in a contrasting color, is sometimes inserted into the seam of the knife edge, giving the pillow a more professional look. A boxed pillow is one that has a welt, or a cord, around the top of the pillow and one around the bottom. The edge of a boxed pillow is a narrow (2 1/2-inch or 3-inch) flat strip of the same fabric. When the top, bottom, side, and welting are all assembled, the pillow has a boxy look, which some designs seem to need. For example, circular pillows often look better when boxed.

When you have decided what kind of design would look best for your particular project, glance through the book to select a design that pleases you. There may be several adaptable to your use. I would most certainly recommend that you read carefully the instructions for Design #1 before setting to work on your first piece, as they are worked out in greater detail than those which follow.

A Word about Yarns

I suppose my favorite words of advice concerning yarn for needlepoint would be "try anything!" Anything and everything. If it doesn't create the effect you desire, rip it out and try something else. It is that simple.

I think the most exciting thing about doing needlepoint is the availability of an endless variety of yarns. When beginning to work at this craft, I noticed most references recommended Persian or tapestry wool. Well, I certainly like to use these wools, as you will see, but I've found I also love the textures of soft matte cotton, perle cotton, and linen, as well as the look of rayon. Using different kinds of yarns *in the same shade* can produce subtle but vibrant surface contrasts in your work. I have used all kinds of yarn, even handspun wool found in a charming shop in Helsinki, where no one spoke English but everyone understood yarns. The search really is more than half the fun.

Certainly I have been disappointed with some of the results. It is necessary to use double strands of delicate or thin threads such as those used in weaving and embroidery, but they add so much to the finished product it is worth the effort. Some specialty shops sell beautifully textured yarns for knitting machines. These yarns are inexpensive and are available in the most elegant colors. Occasionally, I will find a yarn that needs to be used in very short lengths, such as a rayon used in hand-weaving, so that it will not weaken as it is sewn in and out of the canvas. I simply adjust my thinking to how practical the yarn will be and try to use it most effectively. Some yarns, such as metallic or extremely short-fibered threads, may be so fragile as to be only used in the most sparse and decorative way. I have, however, been known to sacrifice texture for color and color for texture.

It is said that cotton embroidery thread loses its sheen. In all likelihood that is true, although I have not found it to be so. There is much cotton used in my work. Silk is rather difficult to handle—it wants to fly apart instead of staying in one smooth thread. Just work patiently and carefully, and your silk stitches will shine with loveliness.

In selecting yarn, consider the purpose of your needlepoint. A pillow will not require the sturdiness of a rug, which should be made of good quality wool. If your work is to be framed, then fragile delicate yarns may be used freely. None of the yarns recommended in the book ran in blocking. Be cautious about the washability of yarns, however, if you are using substitutes, or if you wish to use a needlepoint inset on a garment that will need special washing or cleaning. Be practical, then, but be inventive too.

Whatever yarn you select to use on your needlepoint project, no matter the artistic purpose, it must above all be thick enough to cover the canvas threads, for this is what needlepoint is all about! The terms I have used in the instructions throughout the book, to indicate the thickness required, are simple. When the words *full strand* are used for Persian wool, I mean the 3-ply strand as it comes in the hank. If I use only 1 or 2 of these strands in a design, you must divide the full strand accordingly.

Some of the cottons are 6-ply embroidery threads, and when I say *full strand* for these, I mean the entire 6-ply thread. Sometimes I use them doubled, in which case you must double the full strand as it comes from the package. In certain cases where the Gobelin stitch has been used, triple strands of cotton will be necessary. In no instance have I split the strands of cotton.

A *full strand* of the matte perlita cottons, suede yarn, crewel wool, knitting wool, polyester tapestry yarns, and silk and rayon threads I have used also indicates the yarn as it comes from the hank or package. These yarns are plied, but are seldom split for use on smaller gauged canvas, with the exception of the silk and rayon. I suggest using a full strand or double strand for most of these yarns. But, in the case of the crewel wool, I have sometimes used four strands as they come from the package to create a very thick covering for the canvas.

The wool yarns I have used in these designs, referred to in the instructions as *Persian wool*, are all Paternayan; the numbers refer to colors in their line of wool. If other wools are used, I give their brand names.

Canvas

The canvas I have used for these geometric designs is a white mono canvas, with either 10 threads to the inch (#10 gauge) or 12 threads to the inch (#12 gauge). Mono canvas is generally stiff and sturdy with a slightly shiny surface. As you work with it, it becomes more pliable, but retains a firm resistance against the yarn, giving the backing needed for your work. Buy the best possible quality you can find in canvas. Good materials are never an extravagance. Avoid soft sleazy canvas, for it becomes almost like cheesecloth as you work on it.

I have noticed in working over large areas that although the canvas holes seem square they are slightly rectangular instead and that a true and mathematically accurate square seldom results. So do not expect your work, even though it measures, for example, 80 threads by 80 threads, to be perfectly square. It will appear square to the eye, but not by the ruler.

In selecting canvas for any of these designs, you must consider the many stitches that reach over many canvas threads. Any stitch reaching over 5/8 inch may be too long. Because of my long-reach stitches I have selected a canvas gauge (#10 or #12) that accommodates them nicely, and worked the designs on graph paper with 10 boxes to the inch. You may for some reason wish to use a larger gauge, such as a #5 or #8 canvas. If this is the case, do not select a design with long-reach stitches because there will be long lengths of unattached yarn on the surface of your large-gauge canvas which will catch and snag in use, especially on seat covers or pillows .

On the other hand, you may wish to go to as small a canvas as a #16 or smaller (petit point). If so, the entire design may become very small and you will have to choose thin yarns, perhaps silks or rayons and fine wools, to fit through the small holes. You may want to repeat this entire small motif in a group of four, creating a lovely new design of your own.

As you can see, changing canvas size suggests many variation possibilities. It will also change the size of your piece. The dimensions given with each pattern are for 10- or 12-gauge canvas. If you change the canvas gauge to a *higher* number, your dimensions will be *smaller*; if you change the gauge to a *lower* number your dimensions will be *bigger!*

It is necessary to bind the raw edges of your cut canvas to prevent raveling. Masking tape will eventually work loose at the corners and it looks messy. It will leave a sticky edge on your canvas when you remove it. The most practical binding I have found is a paper tape called Micropore, available in drug stores in many widths. It stays firmly around the canvas edges and because it is white it looks pretty too.

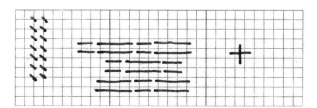

Stitches

Since this whole adventure was brought about by my love affair with needlepoint stitches, I feel I must offer some explanation about the use of those represented in the charts.

Why one stitch looks so marvelous alongside another, or why I use one particular stitch instead of another, I haven't the faintest idea. They just seem to *fit*, and when they are right they do great things on the canvas, lifting the design from the ordinary. If what I have done gives you pleasure, I am indeed gratified.

When you leaf through the pages of charts, you will see that each one has its own stitch diagram. Since I have used some variations of regular stitches you are also given the root, or base stitch from which I have adapted the one to be used in the design. The variation stitch should be sewn in the same basic way as the regular stitch.

I will use the word *background* quite a bit. By background I am referring to the area that surrounds a repeat pattern or a center motif. The background is usually made up of one stitch only. It is often a flat stitch, for the background must serve as the backdrop to the fancy stuff.

In the charts, I do not fill in the complete background stitches. There will be enough of these stitches drawn in to show you the kind, direction, and number needed, as well as any other necessary information. I have not filled out large areas of background to keep the drawings from appearing too complicated. You can see how the background looks in the color picture of each complete design.

I cannot stress the importance of working carefully and neatly. The wrong side of your worked canvas should look as finished as the right side. When ending one yarn, run it under several worked stitches on the wrong side and cut it off *close to the surface*. You don't want the tag ends being pulled through to the front by your new piece of yarn or the adjoining stitches.

Needles

I prefer a #18 tapestry needle for everything except silk and some rayon. For these yarns I use a smaller #20 or #22. Tapestry needles are blunt-tipped. They are easy to thread if you cut a small piece of paper, fold it in half, enclosing the end of the yarn, and thread the paper through the hole in the needle.

Thimble

Yes, you will need to use a thimble. I bought an old silver one on Portobello Road in London years ago. I use it constantly and often wonder about the original owner whose initials, A.C., are engraved on it rather elegantly.

Scissors

I use small sharp embroidery scissors that are antique. I have collected old scissors for a long while, and can't seem to resist a new find.

Of course, there are many fine contemporary thimbles and embroidery scissors that can be purchased in needlepoint shops and department stores. But if an old thimble or pair of scissors is available to you—perhaps your mother's or grandmother's—it somehow seems to increase the pleasure of needlepoint. It's nice to know you are doing something that women have enjoyed for centuries.

Marking Your Canvas

Using these geometric needlepoint charts and counting canvas threads eliminates the need for marking your canvas.

In fact, because I have seen so much beautiful needlepoint completely ruined during the blocking process by supposedly waterproof pens, I am reluctant to touch any canvas with *any* pen. The best way to insure your work against this damage, if mark you must, is to carefully test each pen. Mark a scrap of canvas, let it dry several hours, then dip in water and scrub a bit. If the ink bleeds, do *not* use the pen.

On those occasions when it is absolutely necessary, I have made it a rule to use a pen that most closely matches the color of the yarn I am using. A red pen for red yarn, etc. For white, I use a pale blue pen. And then I scarcely touch the canvas with the pen so that only a tiny dot gives me the mark I need. Make it a habit of yours to avoid excessive pen lines on your canvas, regardless of how waterproof your pens are, because some of the marks may show through the stitches.

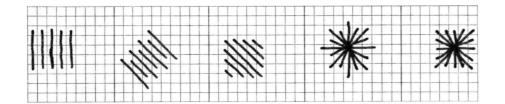

16

Blocking

Working with these charts and the stitches used in these designs will leave your work straight and practically free from distortion. Nevertheless, some blocking is necessary to let the stitches fall into a smooth, neat fabric.

As a milliner, I learned to use a steaming tea kettle for blocking. It's a simple method and most effective. With the steaming tea kettle spout facing out, and your hands carefully away from the steam, hold the outside edge of the canvas so that the stitched part falls in the path of the steam. Pull and stretch, letting the steam play through the worked needlepoint. The yarn will absorb some moisture and the canvas can easily be manipulated. Turn to your ironing board, which you have previously padded well with a clean towel. Place the needlepoint face down on the towel, pull and stretch it straight, and then pin straight down into the edges of the canvas every inch or so through the towel into the ironing board cover. Allow the piece to dry thoroughly, which may take 24 hours or longer. Your work will be blocked when dry.

If you are fortunate enough to own one of those marvelous adjustable blocking frames (Meyer Needlepoint Blocking Device), your needlepoint will be blocked to perfection. Just hook your finished needlepoint over the brass pins according to the instructions, and, with a hand spray bottle filled with water, lightly spray the stretched canvas both from top and bottom. Allow to dry for 24 hours or longer if necessary.

Finishing Information

The pillows have been filled with a separate pillow, or *inner*, made of drapery lining fabric that has in turn been filled with kapok, Dacron, or down. The backing material is given with the instructions for each design, and any other special detail or use of trim is also noted. Design #11 illustrates a method of finishing a pillow with a special needlepoint welt.

The last chapter in the book includes instructions for finishing a handbag, glasses case, and a picture frame, although there are countless other uses for needlepoint.

II. DESIGNS

The Charts

In the following charts I have attempted to present a contemporary series of designs using traditional needlepoint stitches along with variations of some of those stitches. They are geometric in nature, which I find makes them endlessly more interesting. Being geometric, the designs demand accuracy. It is imperative that you count carefully, for the slightest error will produce disastrous results.

So then, since *counting* is the only requirement necessary, we can all relax and enjoy this delightful craft.

Even if you are a beginner in needlepointing, there is no reason to shy away from using the charts. Each line on the graph paper represents a thread on the canvas. Each stitch is carefully charted in an exact location. If a line is drawn across two graph lines, sew your yarn across two canvas threads. Each hole or square on the graph paper represents the identical hole on the canvas. In some instances there may be two or even three different stitches meeting in one square on the chart; then simply sew your stitches into that equivalent hole on the canvas.

The colored pen lines indicate yarn or color changes used in my needlepoint, but, as you will see from the photograph of the piece, the colors on the chart are merely codes which make the graph much easier to read. They are not the same colors I used but are color keyed to those yarn numbers, should you wish to use them. This does not necessarily mean you should follow these color changes or yarn texture changes. Many other variations can be devised.

Center Motif Designs*

On some charts you will be given one quarter of a center design. On others, one half. The black arrows shown at two sides of the chart will always intersect at the *exact* center of each design. Sometimes this exact center will be a canvas hole, other times the center will fall where two canvas threads cross, but it is always marked with a single black dot. The particular stitch that covers this center will be the first stitch you make. So your work will then begin in the center and work out to the outside, following each additional stitch on the chart.

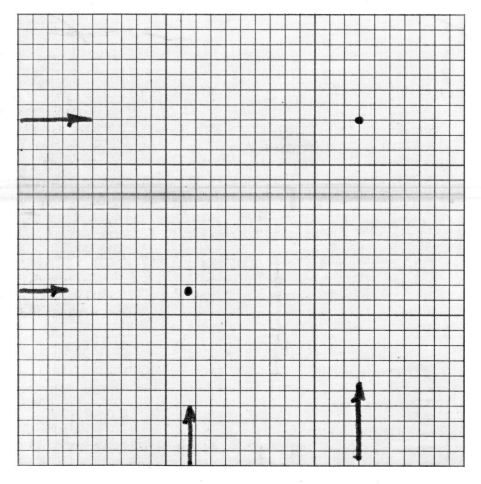

Symbols used on all center motif charts. Sometimes the arrows point to a canvas hole, and sometimes they point to the intersection of two canvas threads.

*Design 1 (color chart), 2, 3, 8, 9, 10, 12, 13, 14, 15, 16, 17 and 19 are center-motif designs.

Repeated Pattern Designs*

On a repeat pattern, you may want to begin your sewing in a corner. This is certainly acceptable. Most of the time, however, I find it more helpful to begin near the center and work out toward the corners in the same manner as the center motif designs. It seems to help me understand the rhythm of each pattern a little better.

My repeat patterns are in most cases made into pillows or cushions. They can be used in so many ways it would be impossible to give examples. Use your imagination and make them work for you and your particular needs.

Using The Charts

Whatever method you select for beginning your needlepoint, you must remember to *count carefully* every thread and every stitch. If you make a mistake, if one stitch fails to fall in exactly the right location next to another, you must count back and take out the work that is wrong. Usually this will be just a few stitches, for you will notice a discrepancy almost immediately. You'll be in good company if you rip a bit; I have never met a needlewoman that didn't do her share. It's easy to miscount.

Each chart is accompanied by special instructions and suggestions. The stitches that make up the design are identified and diagrammed with every chart. If a variation of a particular stitch is used, the stitch from which it was adapted is illustrated and labeled.

As you begin your needlepoint and become familiar with the chart, you will notice that for each stitch a rhythm develops so that you no longer use the chart for reference as often as you did in the beginning. An understanding of the design seems to unfold in the process of the actual sewing. You are more aware of the relationship of the stitches to the total design. It is at this point that true enjoyment of geometric needlepoint starts.

*Design 1 (black-and-white chart), 2 (center), 4, 5, 6, 7, 11, 12 (center), 14 (center), and 18 are repeated-pattern designs.

Let Us Begin Design #1

I have selected Design #1, which is basically a repeat pattern, as an example of a simple square motif. If you follow this step-by-step design procedure, you will better understand all of the charts that follow. Remember that some of the stitches are exactly by the book, so that you may already know them, where others are variations adjusted to fit a particular number of canvas lines or to produce a particular effect.

Keep in mind that every pen line is a type of yarn and every graph line is a canvas thread.

The first chart (1B) is a tile developed through a simple arrangement of our stitches. It is basically a geometric square that has become an interesting pattern of Gobelin stitch, a variation of the eyelet stitch, and a variation of the double leviathan stitch. By *tile* I mean a small unit of the overall pattern, which can be repeated in various ways to form the design.

The stitch key (1A) shows the actual stitches used in the lefthand column and the traditional stitches from which they are derived in the column or columns to the right. The Gobelin stitch is used in its traditional form and that is why no other stitches are shown next to it. The cross-stitch is added after the other stitches, as shown in the next chart (1C), which is a central design developed by grouping two tiles together. The beginning of the third and fourth tile are also shown.

Very careful counting of canvas threads is necessary to insure accuracy. Our tile has become something much more than a simple square. It has taken on the character of numerous squares and triangles, and even appears to have become intricate and complex. But remember, we are still working with just a few basic stitches and the tile is only being repeated to form these geometric patterns.

You might like to make a sample tile from a scrap of canvas. (Trim the canvas off short, or fold it under). After you have completed one tile on your large canvas, move the sample tile about in relation to it, placing it in various positions adjacent to your work. This technique is a valuable tool in developing a design. As one tile fits against the other, stitches create new shapes, and color arrangements often produce delightful results. When you have found a good arangement, you can begin stitching again on the larger canvas.

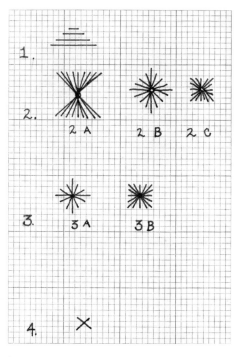

1a

Stitch key for tiles used in Design #1.

1. Gobelin
2. A. Variation of the Eyelet
2. B. Diagonal Eyelet
2. C. Eyelet
3. A. Variation of Double Leviathan
3. B. Double Leviathan
To which we will add:
4. Cross-stitch

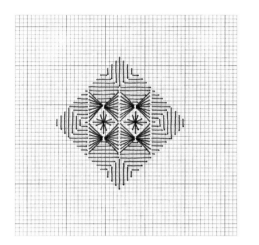

1b

A single repeat, or tile, for the design.

Note the symbol of the black arrow. It points to the exact center of this design. In this case, it is a canvas hole that is covered with a cross-stitch where two tiles meet. If you were to use this pattern, you would have to find the center of your own canvas, by folding it first horizontally and then vertically, and begin sewing with this cross-stitch where your canvas folds cross.

1c

Two tiles with the start of two additional tiles. The arrow points to the exact center of the design.

As we add the third tile motif and then a fourth, and so on around the central cross-stitch, we will be constantly working out toward the edges from this center. A large design based on this simple repetition can be very interesting (1D). Notice that the dimensions of the piece can be varied by adding more tiles in one direction than the other, by adding half a tile, and so forth. The piece is a completely textured design in which the total surface is highly patterned. From this basic design others can be developed, such as the center-motif variation with a basketweave-stitch background that follows. It is shown in a color chart (1E) and color picture (1F). Other very interesting color variations are illustrated on page 27. The stitch key (1G) for the color chart is the same as before, with the addition of basketweave stitch. The smooth texture of this stitch plays excitingly against the texture of the bumpy pattern stitches.

1d

Chart for design composed of a simple repetition of the tiles. This variation is shown in the color picture on page 27, bottom left and right.

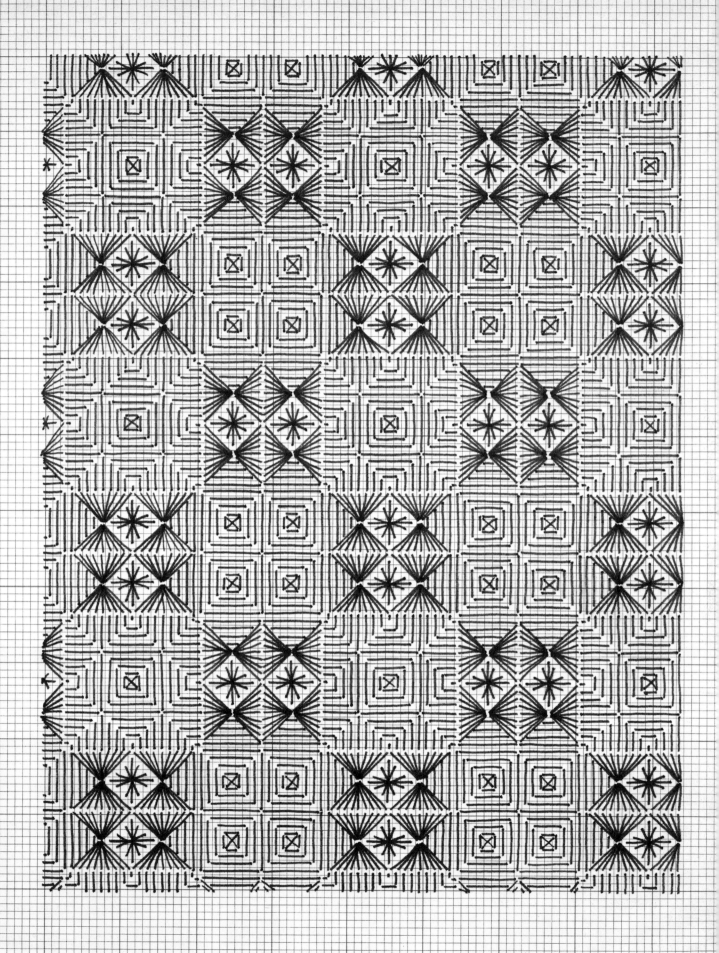

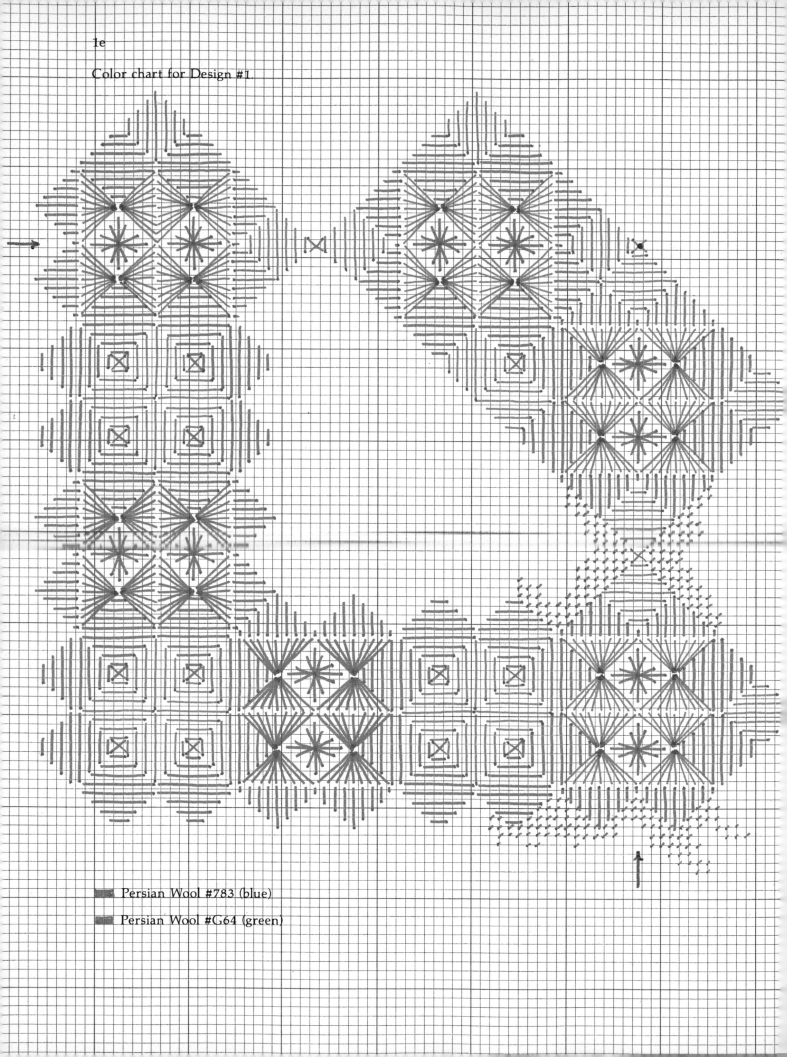

1e

Color chart for Design #1

Persian Wool #783 (blue)

Persian Wool #G64 (green)

Design 1

1f

Design #1. *Summer Shower.*

Variations on Design #1. *Top left:* four tiles meet in the center, and part of the adjacent tiles are "borrowed" for the four beige linen squares. This yarn and the "Caramel" Craftspun Rayon are handweaving yarns that fray easily and should be used in short lengths. *Top right:* four tiles meet in the center, and the color changes within the stitches themselves create the mosaic effect. Persian wools are: #427 (gold), #783 (blue), #308 (navy blue), #520 (green), and #267 (rust). The square is surrounded by one row of navy blue continental stitch. *Bottom left:* an overall repeat in a single color (#852, peach) produces subtle patterning. *Bottom right:* the same repeat in gradations of white (#005), light gray (#168), medium gray (#164), and dark gray (#162) accents the patterns implicit in the design.

Design #1. *Summer Shower*
Pillow, 12" × 12", #12 canvas

Yarns:
Persian Wool #G64 (green)
Persian Wool #783 (blue)
  Use full strand for Gobelin stitches
  Use 2 strands for eyelet stitches
  Use 2 strands for basketweave stitches

Cut your canvas 18 × 18 inches and bind with tape. With your needles and yarn at hand, proceed by lightly folding the canvas in half, then crease it and fold again into quarters. The point where these creases cross will be the center, from which you begin stitching. Remember it is not necessary nor desirable to mark your canvas.

This chart is one quarter of the whole design. By studying the chart you will see that the black arrows point to and intersect at the black dot which marks *exact* center. In this case the dot is a canvas hole that is covered with a cross-stitch sewn over two canvas threads. Turn to your canvas center and make this stitch first. You are ready to sew, carefully counting canvas threads to duplicate those lines on the chart.

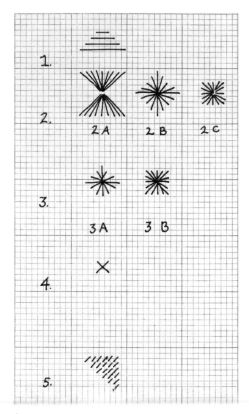

1g

Stitch key for Design #1.
1. Gobelin
2. A. Variation of Eyelet
2. B. Diagonal Eyelet
2. C. Eyelet
3. A. Variation of Double Leviathan
3. B. Double Leviathan
4. Cross-stitch
To which we now add:
5. Basketweave

Note: Leave the variation of the eyelet stitch to last and it will more easily fall right into place.

The chart that is shown is the lower left corner. Since you have been given one quarter of the total design, you must repeat it four times, working from the center out, until your work approximates the full design, which is illustrated in the photograph (1F). After you have completed the geometric design, you will no longer need to refer to the chart. Work the background of basketweave stitch, remembering to allow 3 extra rows around the outside edge for a seam allowance.

By using a matching green linen backing and a blue linen welt, the color scheme of this knife edged pillow is enhanced (see color picture 19 in Chapter III).

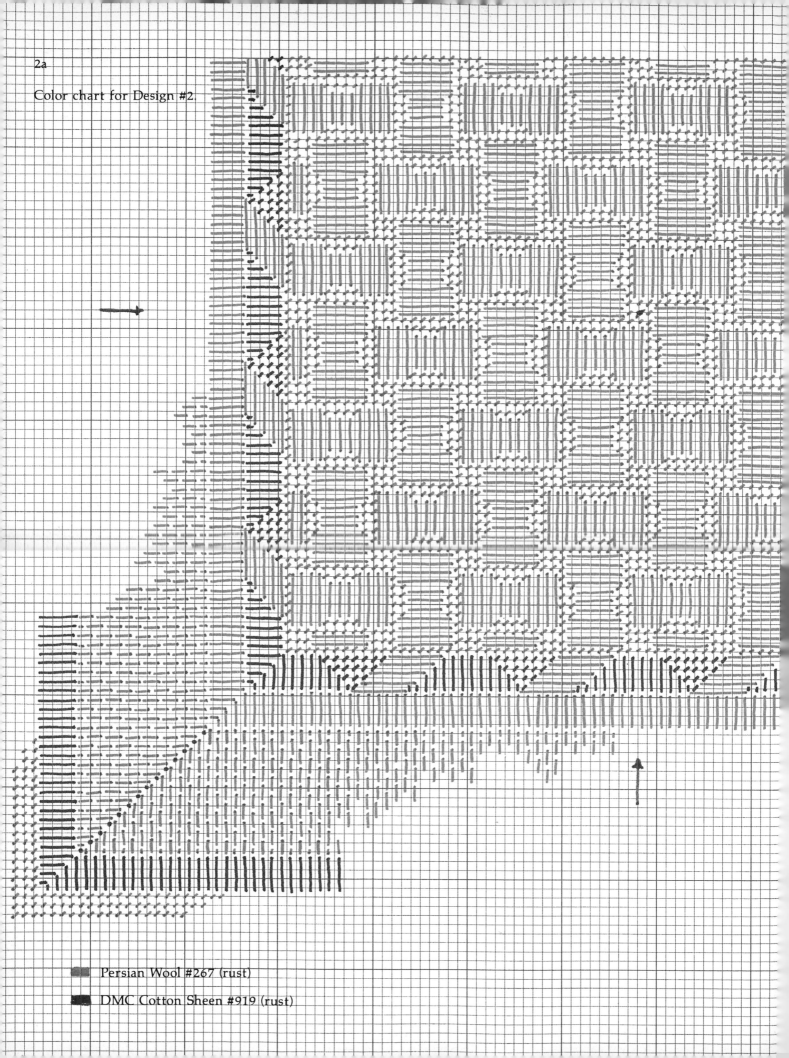

2a

Color chart for Design #2.

Persian Wool #267 (rust)

DMC Cotton Sheen #919 (rust)

Design 2

2b

Design #2. *Ann's Pillow.*

Design #2. *Ann's Pillow*
Pillow, 15" × 15", #12 canvas

Yarns:
Persian Wool #267 (rust)
    Use full strand for Gobelin stitches
    Use full strand for brick stitches
    Use 2 strands for continental stitches
    Use 1 strand for continental-stitch seam allowance
DMC 6-ply Cotton Sheen #919 (rust)
    Use full strand for continental stitches
    Use triple strand for Gobelin stitches

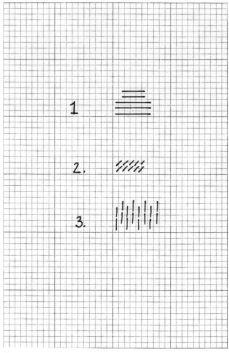

2c

Stitch key for Design #2.
1. Gobelin
2. Continental
3. Brick

This interwoven basket design, using the Gobelin stitch defined by the continental stitch, reaches across 6 canvas threads at the longest point. I have used the design as a center motif of a 6-inch square centered on the canvas and finished with a mitered border of brick stitch. The chart (2A) shows only a narrow portion of the 3 3/4-inch width I have used in my border. You may use any width you prefer.

On the chart you are given slightly more than one quarter of the center motif and the total design, as the black arrows indicate. To begin, cut a piece of canvas 21 × 21 inches. Tape the edges and fold to find the approximate center. The black dot, marking *exact* center, is at the point where two canvas threads cross. It is covered with a continental stitch. Make this stitch first. Then proceed with the surrounding continental stitches, doing these first and then filling in the Gobelin stitches as you go along.

When sewn, this motif gives a basketweave effect, as if the horizontal pattern lines were interlacing with the vertical ones. It would make a handsome repeat pattern by eliminating the border, enlarging the design to cover the entire area, and finishing the design with a simple border of Gobelin stitches in a contrasting yarn. If you choose to use it as a repeat pattern, you must be sure to do this basket motif in units of two, that is an *even* number of rows in both horizontal and vertical directions, in order for the corners and returns to complete the pattern correctly.

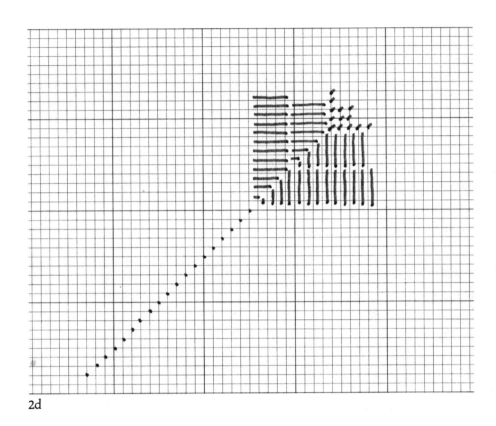

2d

Making the mitered corner effect in Design #2.

Diagonal marking of the canvas is shown in this chart (2D). Note that the diagonal corners are marked on the color chart (2A) by black dots. You may want to mark your own canvas accordingly. After *completing* the center motif, and determining the finished size of your pillow, you should count to the specific row of the width of your border. With a ruler, find the true bias (diagonal) along the line where the canvas threads cross, from corner to corner, as shown.

You will need to mark each of the four corners of your canvas. With a pen that is waterproof (see the cautions on page 16) mark your canvas with a tiny dot very lightly at the point where the threads cross. This line is where your brick stitches meet, giving the mitered finish to the border.

Complete your design by sewing the Gobelin border around the outer edge using the contrasting yarn. Use 4 rows of continental stitch for a seam allowance.

This pillow is backed with linen, knife edged, and finished with a welt (see color picture 13 in Chapter III).

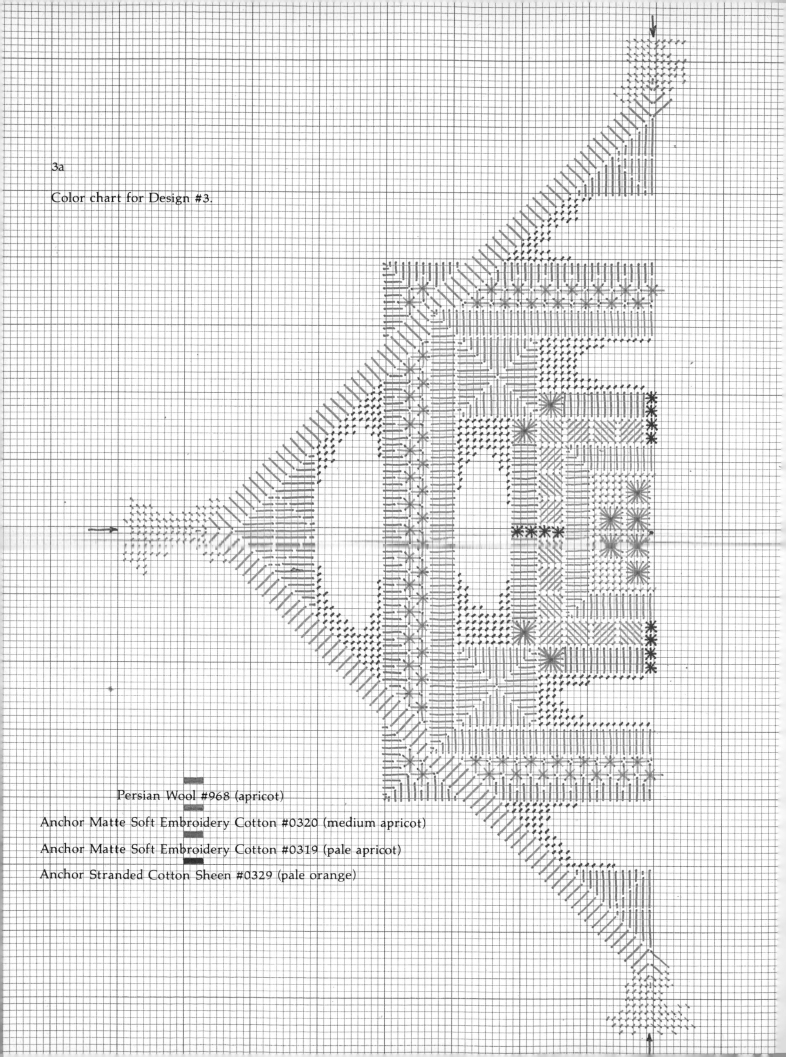

3a

Color chart for Design #3.

Persian Wool #968 (apricot)

Anchor Matte Soft Embroidery Cotton #0320 (medium apricot)

Anchor Matte Soft Embroidery Cotton #0319 (pale apricot)

Anchor Stranded Cotton Sheen #0329 (pale orange)

Design 3

3b

Design #3. *Bittersweet.*

Design #3. *Bittersweet*
Pillow, 14" × 14", #12 canvas

Yarns:
Persian Wool #968 (apricot)
    Use full strand for all pattern stitches
    Use 2 strands for basketweave stitch
    Use 1 strand for continental stitch seam allowance
Anchor Matte Soft Embroidery Cotton #0320* (medium apricot)
Anchor Matte Soft Embroidery Cotton #0319* (pale apricot)
Anchor Stranded Cotton Sheen #0329* (pale orange)
    Use double strands for all pattern stitches
    Use full strand for continental stitches

Since in this case you are given one half of the total design in the chart, you will make a mirror image to complete the whole. Cut your canvas 20 × 20 inches, tape the edges, and fold to find the approximate center. On the chart, exact center is marked with a black dot in a canvas hole where 4 double leviathan stitches meet. Begin your work by doing these stitches first.

Continue to form the crosslike design in the center made by these double leviathan stitches. Surround them with a matte cotton ground of continental stitch and you are well on your way. Carefully refer to the chart for yarn changes, for the cottons are very close in color value. You will be rewarded with a most subtly beautiful design. Continue working one concentric square border after the other, building out from the center. If you prefer, the continental stitches may be filled in last, after establishing each consecutive square of "border" stitches.

*These yarns were purchased in London and their numbers may differ from Anchor yarn exported to the United States. Refer to the color illustration (3B) and color names when selecting your cottons.

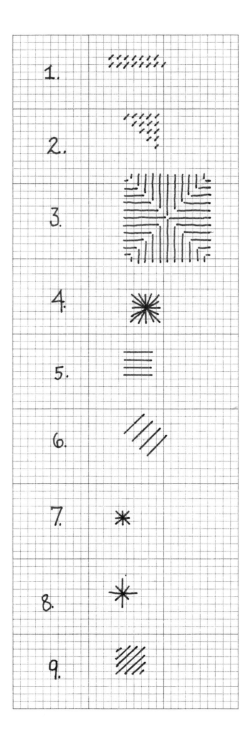

Take care that the direction of the *last thread* you sew in the double straight cross-stitches and the double leviathan stitches are consistent in direction. As you can see in the stitch key (3C) these two stitches are made by several threads crossing over one another. The photograph (3B) shows the highly textured surface achieved, and that the final or top threads in the stitches in the horizontal rows are horizontally placed, while the final threads in the vertical rows are vertically placed.

When the center design is finished, sew the basketweave background, but first note on the chart (3A) how its direction changes at each apex of the design. Complete your pillow with 3 rows of continental stitch for a seam allowance.

The pillow is finished with a color-matched linen for a welted knife edge (see color picture 8 in Chapter III). This delightful design is one of my favorites. I can imagine it bordering an area rug, in closely related shades of gray on white, or perhaps browns and black with beige.

3c

Stitch key for Design #3.
1. Continental
2. Basketweave
3. Triangle
4. Double Leviathan
5. Gobelin
6. Slanted Gobelin
7. Smyrna Cross-stitch
8. Double Straight Cross-stitch
9. Scotch

Color chart for Design #4.

Handspun Wool from Finland (gold)

Persian Wool #452 (yellow)   Pearsall Silk Filo-Floss #151 (yellow)

Design 4

4b

Design #4. *Sunflower.*

Design #4. *Sunflower*
Pillow, 13 1/2″ × 15 1/2″, #12 canvas

Yarns:
Persian Wool #452 (yellow)
    Use full strand for all pattern stitches
    Use 1 strand for continental-stitch seam allowance
Handspun Wool from Finland* (gold)
    Use double strand
Pearsall Silk Filo-Floss #151 (yellow)
    Use double strand

This repeat pattern is most simple to do even though it looks quite complicated. It consists of only two stitches, the triangle stitch and an extended cashmere stitch.

Before sewing, read the instructions *carefully*. In order to understand the mathematical sequence of this design, study the photograph (4B). You will notice that the gold-colored triangle stitches run diagonally across the canvas. Count these lines of triangle stitches, beginning in the upper left corner with: 1 stitch, 4 stitches, then 7, 10, 13, 16, and 16 stitches at the two longest diagonals.

No matter what the dimensions you choose, when you reach the desired width you will have two rows that are the same diagonal length, 16 and 16 in the photograph, and 7 and 7 on the chart. The first of these central rows will form one diagonal corner, the second will form the other. Glance down the right side of the design (4B) from the upper right corner to the lower right and the sequence reads the same: 16, 13, 10, 7, 4, and 1, *in reverse order*, subtracting 3 each time.

This pattern must always fall in the same mathematical sequence. For example, if you prefer a longer and wider pillow, beginning at the top left corner and reading across to the right corner, the sequence would be: 1, 4, 7, 10, 13, 16, 19, 22, and then 22 again. Now down the right side it is: 19, 16, 13, 10, 7, 4, and 1. Always add 3 to increase, do two rows the same at the full width (22 and 22 in this case) and subtract 3 to decrease.

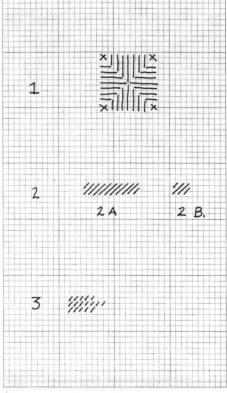

4c

Stitch key for Design #4.
1. Triangle
2. A. Extended Cashmere
2. B. Cashmere
3. Continental

*Closest Persian wool color: #Y50. Use 2 strands.

By the same measuring system you can make the pattern smaller by stopping at perhaps 13 triangle stitches: 1, 4, 7, 10, 13, another 13, 10, 7, 4, and 1, to the lower right corner.

Should you desire to make the pillow wider only, rather than wider and longer, when you reach the proper depth simply do as many rows as you need of the same number. For example, from the upper left corner: 1, 4, 7, 10, 13, 16, 16, 16, and then down the right side to the lower right corner: 13, 10, 7, 4, and 1.

You may plan to use this motif in its simplest repeat form by eliminating the border detail and the fancy corners. Then, of course, you may use any number of triangle stitches in a row.

Now that you have read the instructions, cut a piece of canvas 20 × 22 inches and tape the edges. Start your sewing about 3 inches in from the upper right corner of the canvas and make the first triangle stitch. Surround it with the extended cashmere stitch, as shown on the chart, but remember that the chart is really an abbreviated version of the full pattern, because space did not permit drawing it to the full width of the 16-stitch diagonal. Continue working diagonally across your canvas until you complete that whole row of 16. You have thus established the *upper right corner point* of this design.

Next, sewing to the left of your row of triangle stitches, do the other extended cashmere stitches in the yarns suggested. Now, work the second row of 16 triangle stitches. This row forms the *lower left corner point* of the design. Proceed step by step to work to the upper left corner and in the same manner work to the lower right corner.

Finish your needlepoint with 4 rows of continental stitch for a seam allowance. The pillow is finished with a welted knife edge and is backed with linen (see color picture 7 in Chapter III). The tassels are 3 1/2 inches long and are made of a combination of two wools. I eliminated the silk because it tends to fly away and become quite shaggy looking.

Color chart for Design #5.

Persian Wool #829 (deep pink)

Persian Wool #005 (white)

Design 5

5b

Design #5. *Viking Key.*

Design #5. *Viking Key*
Hearth cushion, 25 1/2" × 14 1/2", #12 canvas

Yarns:
Persian Wool #829 (deep pink)
   Use full strand for Gobelin stitches
Persian Wool #005 (white)
   Use full strand for Gobelin stitches
   Use 1 strand for continental-stitch seam allowance.

This lovely key design was adapted from an ancient textile fragment on display in the Viking Museum in Oslo, Norway. The fabric was one of many discovered in those sweepingly elegant Viking ships once used as royal tombs. As a repeat pattern this is easy to sew, as it uses only one pattern stitch, the Gobelin.

Cut your canvas into a piece 32 × 20 inches and tape the edges. Begin to sew 3 inches in from the outer edge in a corner. Using the main color, I prefer to establish the key repeat in a row up the canvas until the desired size is reached. Cover the canvas with this pattern, and then fill in the background as indicated on the chart.

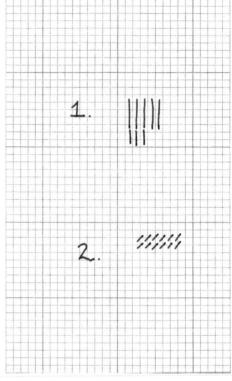

Stitch key for Design #5.
1. Gobelin
2. Continental

This design is most striking when there is a wide contrast between the color of the two yarns. For a much more subtle and equally handsome piece you might select close shades of blue on gray or plum. You could choose to do every other row of keys in a slightly darker tone for variation.

Use 4 rows of continental stitch for a seam allowance. This cushion is finished with a 2-inch boxed edge of linen in a color matching the yarn color of the key motif (see color picture 9 in Chapter III).

Color chart for Design #6.

Persian Wool #365 (navy blue)

Opal Spun Knitting Wool #3206 (navy blue)

Persian Wool #225 (rust)

Design 6

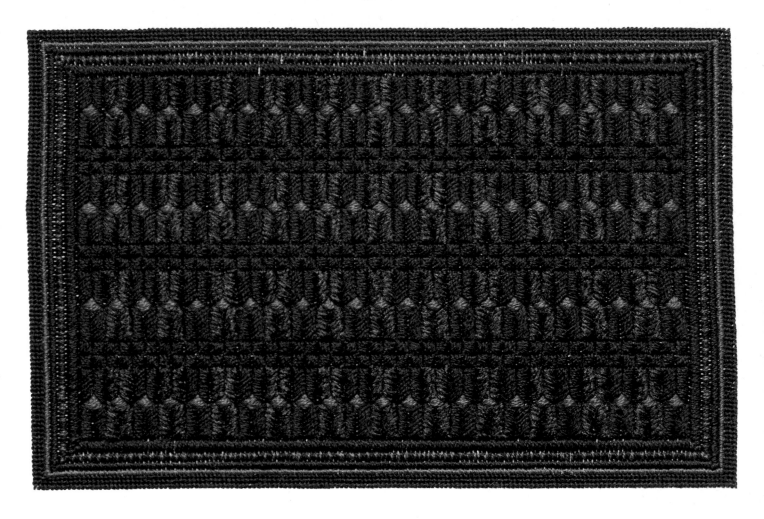

6b

Design #6. *Starry Night.*

Design #6. *Starry Night*
Pillow, 10″ × 15″, #10 canvas

Yarns:
Persian Wool #365 (navy blue)
    Use full strand for all pattern stitches
    Use 1 strand for continental-stitch seam allowance
Persian Wool #225 (rust)
    Use full strand for all stitches
Opal Spun Knitting Wool #3206 (navy blue)
    Use full strand for slanted Gobelin stitch

After binding your 16 × 20 inch canvas with tape, begin sewing the extended cashmere stitches about 3 inches from the edge. Since the Persian wool alternates with the knitting wool, you might like to keep two needles threaded and work with both yarns to develop the pattern. I think it is easier this way.

Fill in the double straight cross-stitches after finishing the first complete row of extended cashmere stitches. Do the two rows of alternating Scotch stitches, and repeat. The pattern is comprised of these two simple steps, and is repeated until you have the size you desire.

I prefer the subtle texture changes of the two wools, but you might like to experiment with different colors as well as textures.

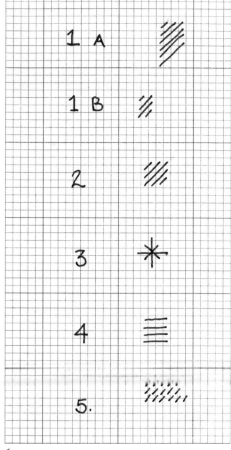

6c

Stitch key for Design #6.
1. A. Extended Cashmere
1. B. Cashmere
2. Scotch
3. Double Straight Cross-stitch
4. Gobelin
5. Continental

There are four borders of varying widths framing this interesting pattern. Note that in the second border of Gobelin stitches I have combined both colors of Persian wool in making up my full 3-ply sewing strand to give an added touch of spice. I have used *2 strands* of navy and *1 strand* of rust.

Complete your needlepoint with 4 rows of continental stitch for sewing because you will want the detail of the borders to show. This pillow has a 2-inch box of linen in navy blue with red welting trim to match the yarn stars (see color picture 16 in Chapter III).

Color chart for Design #7.

Persian Wool #005 (white)   Persian Wool #445 (gold)   Persian Wool #434 (orange)

Persian Wool #Y56 (yellow)   Persian Wool #545 (green)

Design 7

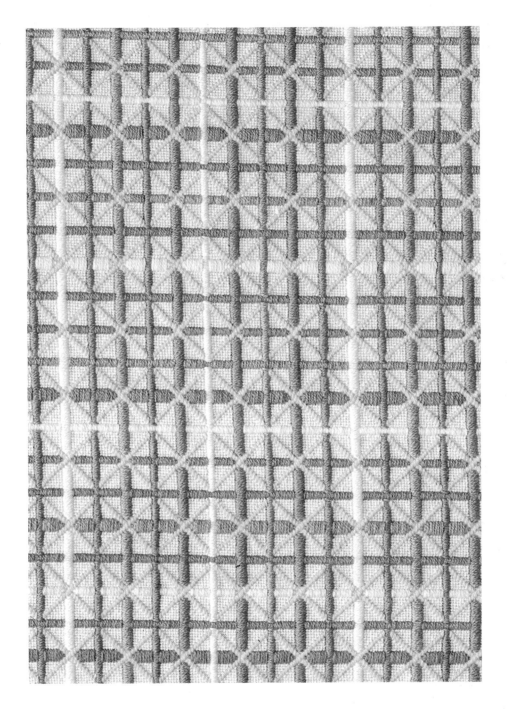

7b

Design #7. *Plaid for a Bamboo Chair.*

Design #7. *Plaid for a Bamboo Chair*
Chair seat, 24" × 28", #12 canvas

Yarns:
Persian Wool:
  #005 (white)
  #Y56 (yellow)
  #434 (orange)
  #445 (gold)
  #545 (green)
  Use full strand for Gobelin stitches
  Use 2 strands for basketweave stitches

Most important in developing a plaid is the selection of colors and their final arrangement. My color grid runs the same from back to front and from right to left in this order:
  White
  Orange
  Gold
  Green
  Orange

Arrange your colors with care. You may decide to do a sample or two just to see how you want them to look, before you start your needlepoint. Plan your background with equal care. It is not necessary to limit yourself to one color as I have done. These basketweave stitches could be arranged to run in one color across every other section for a striped effect, or you might get very fancy and work out another complete shadow plaid in the background, both horizontally and vertically, changing color when both cross. Experiment!

After the final decision is made on your colors, cut a large piece of canvas (mine measured 38 × 34 inches) and tape the edges. Now work in the following order.

1. Establish the Gobelin stitch diagonals, *counting very carefully*. Once these important stitches are in their proper place, the others fall in order easily. (These are the blue diagonals on your chart).

2. Next, follow with the vertical rows (those running from front to back of the seat). You will notice the number of canvas threads over which you sew the Gobelin stitches varies in this way: over 4, then 3, 4, 3, etc.

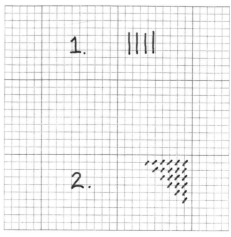

7c

Stitch key for Design #7.
1. Gobelin
2. Basketweave

3. Finish the plaid pattern by doing the horizontal rows. They, too, are varied but in this way: over 5, over 3, 3, 3, and repeat.

4. Fill in the basketweave background.

For finishing the chair seat get professional services, unless you know about upholstery. Finish the seat by gluing a double welted cord over the staples (see photograph and color picture 22 in Chapter III.)

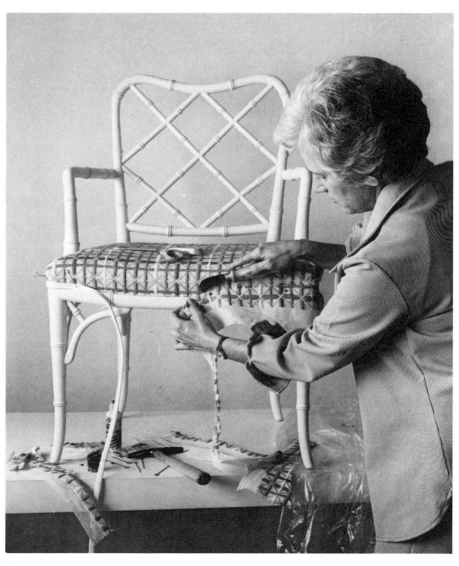

Mrs. Lee Pierce is shown trimming the plaid needlepoint that has been used to cover the chair seat. A double welted cord of white linen, at the left, is to be glued over the staples and forms a neat finish. (Photograph by Chris Edmonds.)

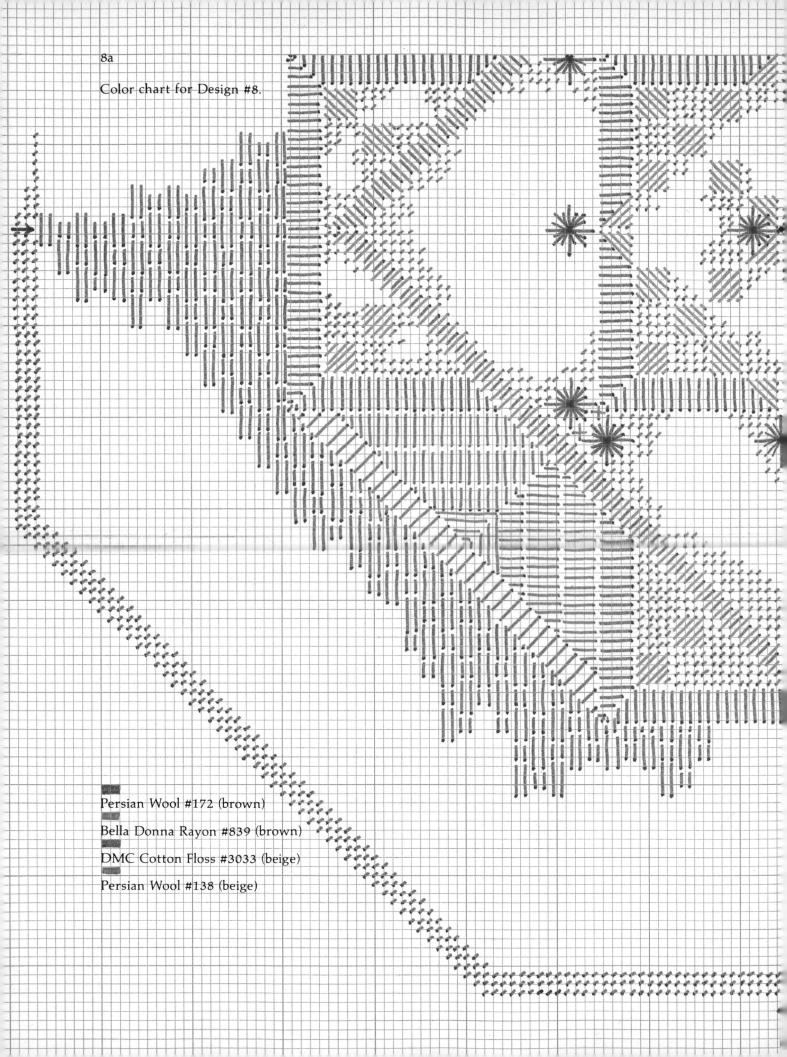

8a

Color chart for Design #8.

Persian Wool #172 (brown)

Bella Donna Rayon #839 (brown)

DMC Cotton Floss #3033 (beige)

Persian Wool #138 (beige)

Design 8

8b

Design #8. *Mariner's Compass.*

Design #8. *Mariner's Compass*
Octagon pillow, 14" across, #12 canvas

Yarns:
Persian Wool #172 (brown)
   Use full strand for all pattern stitches
   Use 1 strand for continental-stitch seam allowance
Persian Wool #138 (beige)
   Use full strand for all pattern stitches
   Use 2 strands for basketweave stitch
Bella Donna Rayon #839 (brown)
   Use double strand for all stitches
DMC Cotton Floss #3033 (beige)
   Use double strand for all stitches

The exact center of this design on the chart is marked by a black dot covering a canvas hole where 2 double leviathan stitches and 2 half Scotch stitches meet. After folding your taped 20 × 20 inch canvas into quarters to find the approximate center, make these 4 stitches first.

Work out from the center, doing the Scotch stitches and the first border of Gobelin stitches. Fill in the basketweave stitches with the cotton floss. Proceed to work each area out from the center in turn until the design is completed.

8c

Stitch key for Design #8.
1. Basketweave
2. Gobelin
3. Slanting Gobelin
4. Scotch
5. A. Variation of the Double Leviathan
5. B. Double Leviathan
6. Upright Cross-stitch
7. Old Florentine
8. Continental

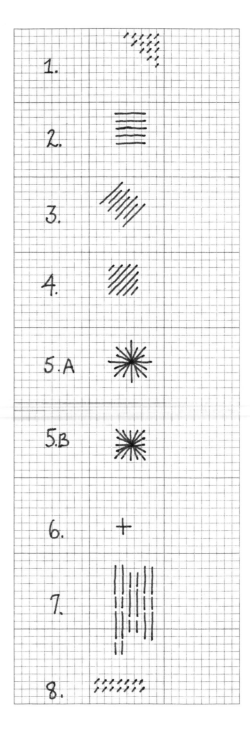

To do the old Florentine border, begin at the left side of your center motif and work out toward the edge, counting stitches carefully, as shown on the chart. Continue working these two stitches, over 4 threads and then over 2 threads to make the old Florentine textured frame that encircles the center.

Finish your pillow with 3 rows of continental stitch on the straight grain of your canvas as usual, but 4 rows on the bias (see chart 8A), for a seam allowance. This pillow is finished with a 2-inch box and backing of antique satin (see color picture 20 in Chapter III).

9a

Color chart for Design #9.

Persian Wool #610 (purple)

Persian Wool #137 (pale purple)

Polyester Tapestry yarn #139 (purple)

Persian Wool #117 (grayish purple)

Design 9

9b

Design #9. *Tangleberry.*

Design #9. *Tangleberry*
Pillow, 15 1/2" × 15 1/2", #12 canvas

Yarns:
Persian Wool #610 (purple)
   Use full strand for Gobelin stitch
   Use full strand for cross-stitch
   Use 2 strands for rice stitch
   Use 2 strands for mosaic stitch
   Use 1 strand for continental-stitch seam allowance
Persian Wool #137 (pale purple)
   Use full strand for Gobelin stitch
   Use 2 strands for rice stitch
   Use 2 strands for basketweave stitch
Persian Wool #117 (grayish purple)
   Use full strand for Gobelin stitch
   Use full strand for Scotch stitch
   Use 2 strands for basketweave stitch
Polyester Tapestry Yarn #139 (purple)
   Use full strand for all stitches

Since you are given slightly more than one quarter of the whole design (9A), make sure to follow the direction of the black arrows to where they meet at the black dot that marks the exact center of the design. This dot covers a canvas hole that is in turn covered by a rice stitch. Cut a piece of canvas 21 × 21 inches, fold it to find the approximate center, and make this rice stitch first. Change yarns to form the crosslike motif that surrounds this rice stitch. Again changing yarns as suggested by the chart, continue working out from the center.

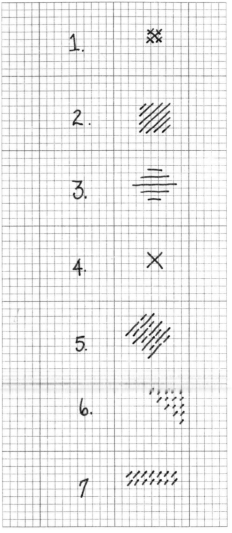

9c

Stitch key for Design #9.
1. Rice
2. Scotch
3. Gobelin
4. Cross-stitch
5. Mosaic
6. Basketweave
7. Continental

After completing the center motif, carefully note the direction of the mosaic stitches in the background; they change at the center of each side. I am particularly fascinated by the interesting way this textural diagonal rib repeats the inner square of Persian wool and heightens the geometric feeling in a subtle way.

Finish your needlepoint with 3 rows of continental stitch for a seam allowance. This pillow is finished in a lovely shade of purple to match the polyester yarn. It has a knife edge and backing of velveteen, with a welt cord (see color picture 14 in Chapter III).

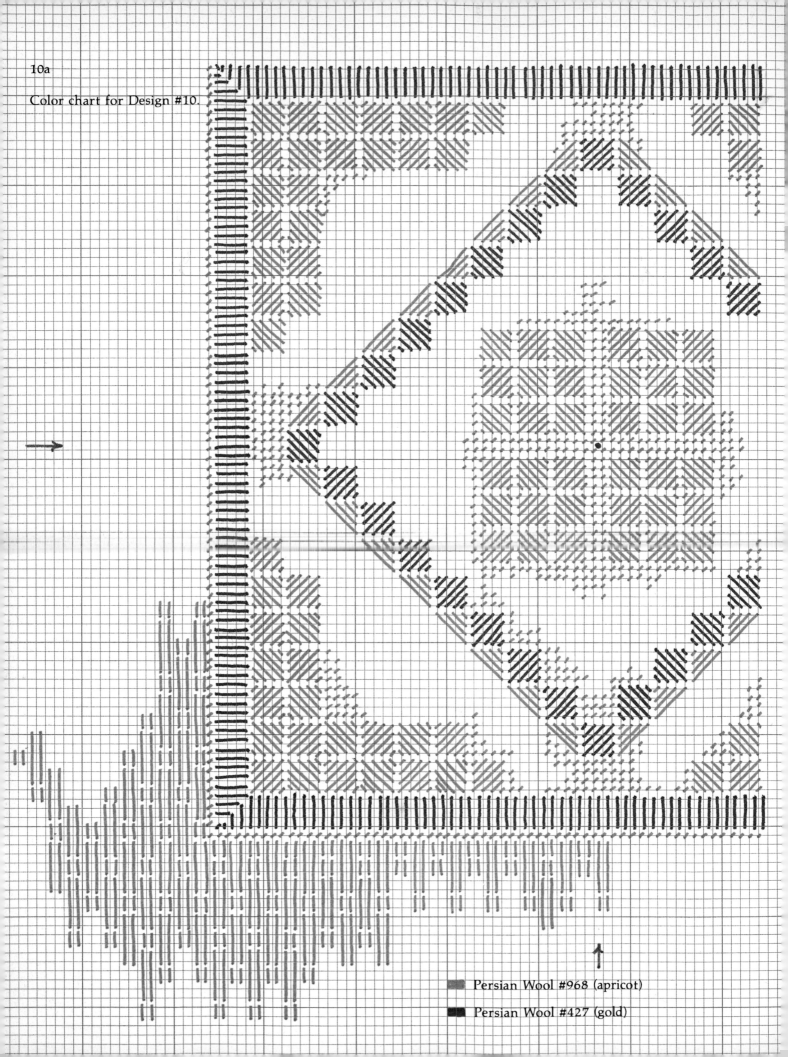

10a

Color chart for Design #10.

Persian Wool #968 (apricot)

Persian Wool #427 (gold)

Design 10

10b

Design #10. *Hop Scotches.*

Design #10. *Hop Scotches*
Pillow, 15" × 15", #10 canvas

Yarns:
Persian Wool #968 (apricot)
   Use full strand for all pattern stitches
   Use 1 strand for continental-stitch seam allowance
Persian Wool #427 (gold)
   Use full strand for all stitches.

This design is charted to give you slightly more than one half of the center motif. It is, however, marked with black arrows to indicate one quarter of the total design. The arrows intersect at the black dot which marks the exact center. This center is located in a canvas hole where 2 continental stitches meet.

After preparing your canvas, which should measure 20 × 20 inches, with taped edges, fold to find the approximate center. Sew the 2 central continental stitches first. Now, work the 2 rows of continental stitches that form the cross dividing the squares of Scotch stitches.

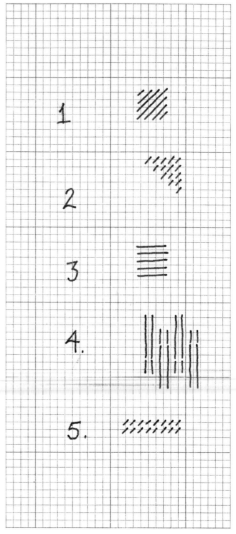

10c

Stitch key for Design #10.
1. Scotch
2. Basketweave
3. Gobelin
4. Old Florentine
5. Continental

Continue sewing out from the center, and finish the large square of Gobelin stitches with one row of continental stitch. Now you are ready to begin the background of old Florentine stitches. Start this textured stitch in the lower left corner of your square exactly as indicated on the chart. This pattern forms a continuous border surrounding the center design.

Finish your pillow with 3 rows of continental stitch for a seam allowance. Corduroy fabric in gold to accent the Persian wool is used to back the pillow and form a welt (see color picture 5 in Chapter III).

Color chart for Design #11.

■ Persian Wool #005 (white)

▬ Bella Donna Rayon (white)

Design 11

11b

Design #11. *Coronet.*

Design #11. *Coronet*
Pillow, 16" × 16" (finished with a special needlepoint welt),
#12 Canvas

Yarns:
Persian Wool #005 (white)
  Use full strand for Gobelin stitch
  Use 1 strand combined with rayon for woven effect and
  border.
Bella Donna Rayon: White (white)
  Use full strand combined with wool for woven effect and
  border

This repeat pattern is one that requires careful counting. It
is such a beautiful design when finished that I find it well
worth while. The diagonal lines that run through the pattern
appear to be laced over and under one another in a woven
"basketweave" effect.

Cut your canvas 22 × 22 inches and tape the edges. You will
begin your needlepoint in the lower left corner. Do the
diagonal lines first, using the combined rayon and wool yarns.
Then, with accurate counting, make the wool square motif and
surround it with the rayon and wool border. You may certainly begin your work in the center of your needlepoint
canvas if you prefer. It is necessary, though, to do only one
square at a time and then surround it with the woven motif.
You will, therefore, be working both square and border together before moving to the next square. Note the directional
change of the rows of squares, which are stitched horizontally
and vertically in alternation. I like to cover the total surface of
the canvas with the bordered squares, before going back and
filling in those little half squares around the outside edge.

Finish your needlepoint with the Gobelin border, over 5
canvas threads as shown on the chart (11A), using the combined rayon and wool yarns. This border becomes your needlepoint welting. You will not finish this pillow with the usual
3 rows of Continental stitch for a seam allowance. It is not
necessary with this method of welting (see color picture 6 in
Chapter III).

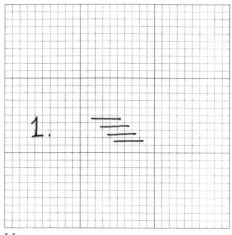

11c

Stitch key for Design #11.

1. Gobelin

Needlepoint Welting with a Gobelin Border

Making a welt with needlepoint is an interesting detail you may want to use on almost any piece of needlepoint that requires a knife edge. It certainly comes in handy when I am using a yarn color that is difficult to match with fabric. In this instance, we want to have a continuation of the shiny textured welting to carry out the design.

Back and stuff your pillow as you usually do, sewing the fabric backing on the very edge of your Gobelin border around the outside as shown in the border detail. White linen is used here. Stuff and hand sew the closing. Now, on the needlepoint side of the pillow, top stitch by machine, sewing on the line of canvas holes where the squares stop and the Gobelin border begins.

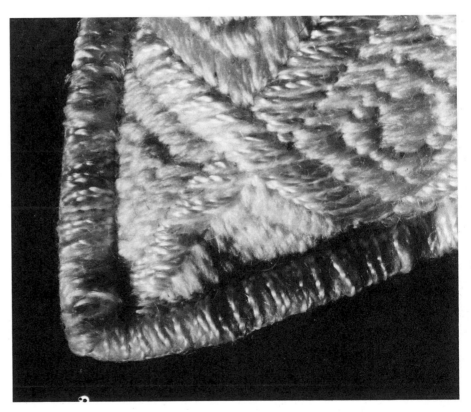

Corner detail of stitching showing needlepoint welting for Design #11.

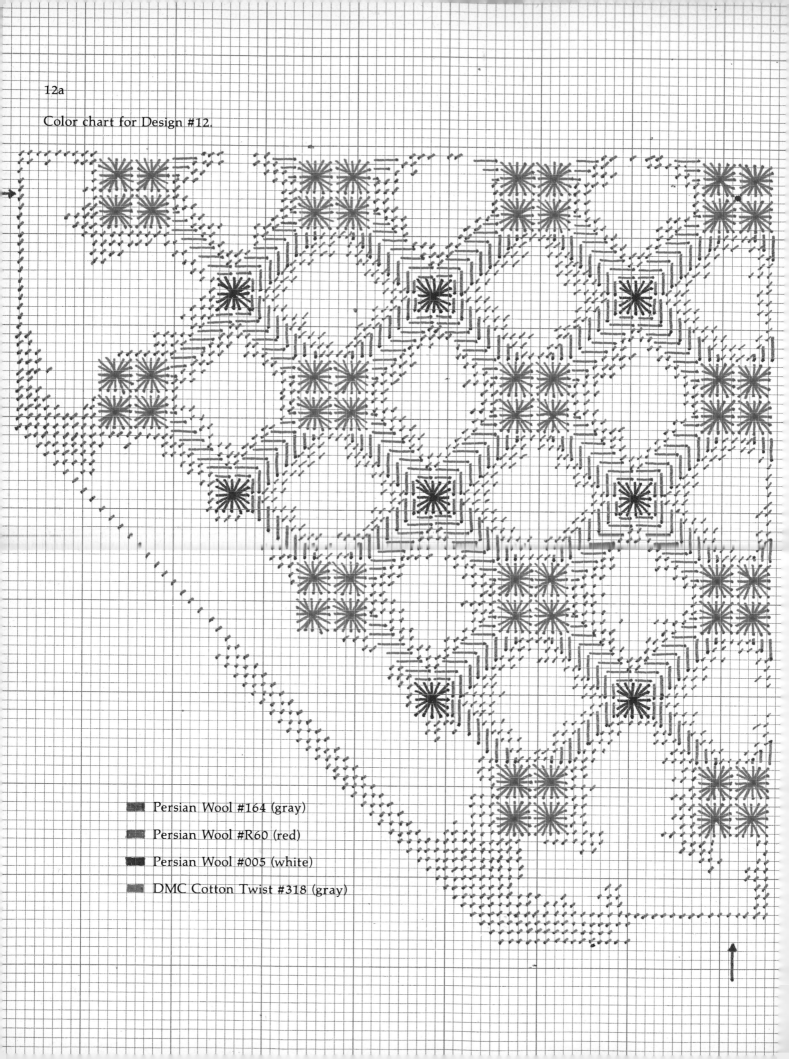

12a

Color chart for Design #12.

Persian Wool #164 (gray)

Persian Wool #R60 (red)

Persian Wool #005 (white)

DMC Cotton Twist #318 (gray)

Design 12

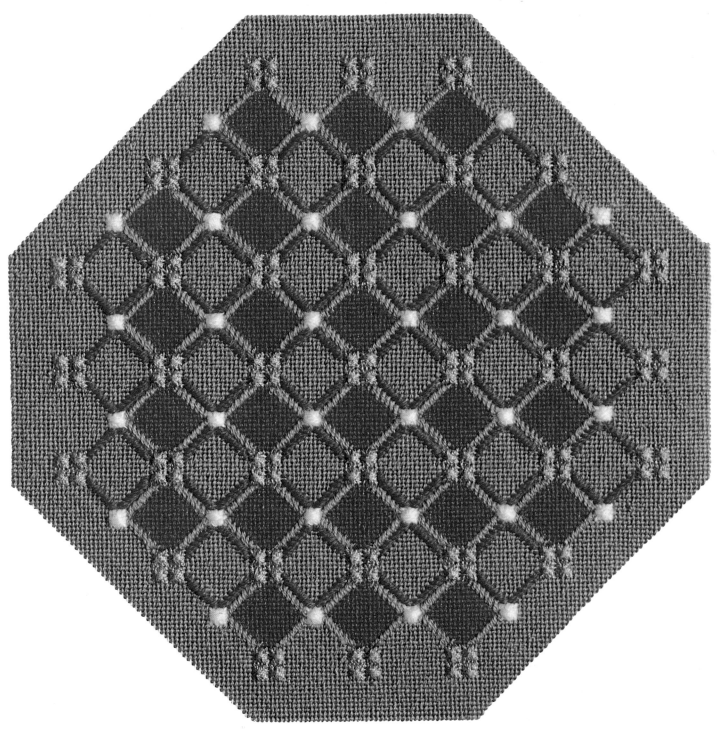

12b

Design #12. *Snowflakes.*

Design #12. *Snowflakes*
Octagon pillow, 13" across, #12 canvas

Yarns:
Persian Wool #164 (gray)
    Use full strand for Gobelin stitch
    Use 2 strands for basketweave stitch
    Use 1 strand for continental stitch
Persian Wool #R60 (red)
    Use full strand for Gobelin stitch
    Use 2 strands for basketweave stitch
Persian Wool #005 (white)
    Use full strand for double leviathan stitch
DMC Cotton Twist #318 (gray)
    Use double strand for double leviathan

On the chart, slightly more than one quarter of the total design is given. The exact center of this design is marked by a black dot in the canvas hole where 4 double leviathan stitches meet. Prepare your canvas, which should measure 19 × 19 inches, by taping the edges and folding into quarters to find the approximate center. You will begin your sewing here, using the cotton floss. Work out from the center, carefully counting stitches and changing yarns. It is important that the last thread of each of the double leviathan stitches (the one that will be on top) goes in the same direction.

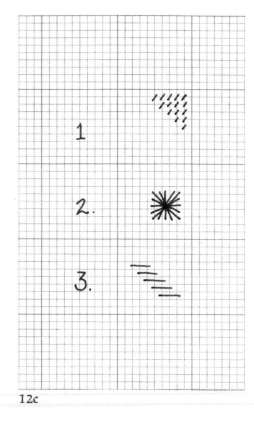

12c

Stitch key for Design #12.
1. Basketweave
2. Double Leviathan
3. Gobelin

I work the basketweave centers as I go along. This is a very easy pattern to do and can be extended on and on for large pieces of needlepoint. It looks lovely in squares of rust and blue with beige accents.

Complete your needlepoint with 3 rows of continental stitch for a seam allowance. Note that on the bias, as shown on the chart, 4 rows are needed, in order to keep the ruler measurement of the seam allowance the same.

This pillow has a 1 1/2-inch boxed edge of gray wool flannel backing and a red cotton trim to match the bright red yarn in the design (see color picture 18 in Chapter III).

13a

Color chart for Design #13.

Persian Wool #242 (red)

DMC Stranded Cotton Sheen #666 (red)

DMC Stranded Cotton Sheen #350 (red)

Appleton Crewel Wool #501 (red)

Design 13

13b

Design #13. *Paprika.*

Design #13. *Paprika*
Pillow, 15″ × 15″, #12 canvas

Yarns:
Persian Wool #242 (red)
  Use full strand for all pattern stitches
  Use 2 strands for basketweave stitch
DMC Stranded Cotton Sheen #666 (red)
  Use double strand for all stitches
DMC Stranded Cotton Sheen #350 (red)
  Use double strand for all stitches
Appleton Crewel Wool #501 (red)
  Use 4 strands for all stitches

The center motif is diagrammed in the chart (13A), where you have been given slightly more than one half of the design. The black arrows point to the exact center, which is marked by a black dot indicating a canvas hole covered by an upright cross-stitch. Fold your 20 × 20 inch piece of canvas, after taping the edges. Find the approximate center and make this upright cross-stitch first.

Change yarns and do the next half Scotch stitches that surround the center stitch. Continue working out from the center, noting yarn and stitch changes. Follow the chart faithfully and count carefully. The design is lots of fun to sew—watch how stitch after stitch dovetails into place.

13c

Stitch key for Design #13.
1. Basketweave
2. Triangle
3. Gobelin
4. Slanting Gobelin
5. Scotch or Milanese
6. Upright Cross-stitch
7. Cross-stitch
8. Smyrna Cross-stitch

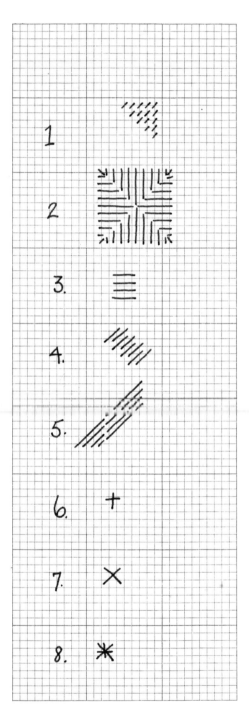

I seem to prefer doing these intricate patterns in a monochromatic color scheme, but you should not limit yourself in the same way. Experiment with lots of colors and lots of yarn textures until you find the combination that pleases you most.

Note the directional change of the last thread of the Smyrna stitches, and the directional change of the background basketweave stitch. Make your pillow as large or small as you like. No need to add additional stitches for a seam allowance, just be sure you figure for the loss of about 3 rows in the overall outside measurement.

This pillow is backed with linen, selected to pick up one of the many tones of red in the design (see color picture 15 in Chapter III).

14a

Color chart for Design #14.

▨ Persian Wool #124 (brown)

▨ DMC Cotton Perle #640 (taupe)

Design 14

14b

Design #14. *Shadows.*

Design #14. *Shadows*
Pillow, 13″ × 13″, #12 canvas

Yarns:
Persian Wool #124 (brown)
    Use full strand for double leviathan stitch
    Use full strand for Gobelin stitch
    Use 2 strands for upright cross-stitch
    Use 1 strand for continental-stitch seam allowance
DMC Cotton Perle #640 (taupe)
    Use double strand for all stitches

You have been given one quarter of the total design on the chart. Black arrows point to the exact center, marked with a black dot, which is a canvas hole where 4 double leviathan stitches meet. Fold your taped 19 × 19 inch canvas to find the approximate center and sew these 4 stitches first, making sure the last thread of each stitch goes in the same direction.

Change your yarn to the cotton perle and surround that group of 4 stitches with the 3 rows of upright cross-stitch. Note carefully that the last thread of the stitch, unlike the double leviathan stitches, changes direction. This directional change is marked on the chart with the *heavy* brown line, which is sometimes shown as a horizontal and sometimes as a vertical stitch. Continue sewing out from the center in the same manner until the crosslike center motif is completed. Work the Gobelin border in wool.

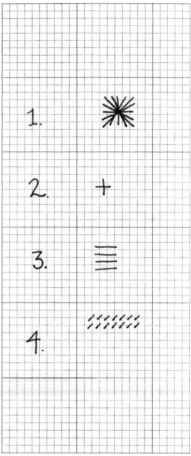

14c

Stitch key for Design #14.
1. Double Leviathan
2. Upright Cross-stitch
3. Gobelin
4. Continental

Count very carefully the number of upright cross-stitches out from the center to the corner designs. Sew them with equal care. These cross-stitches between the center and corner motifs do *not* change the direction of the top thread, which remains consistent. At the corners work the Gobelin stitches first, then the 3 rows of upright cross-stitches, changing the direction of the top thread as indicated. Do the double leviathan stitches and continue until each corner is completed.

Repeating the use of cotton perle in the final border gives a nice finish to this interesting geometric design. Work 4 rows of continental stitch instead of the usual 3 rows. This wider seam allowance gives room for your border to show. The pillow is finished with a 2 inch boxed side in a lovely shade of taupe linen (see color picture 21 in Chapter III).

15a

Color chart for Design #15.

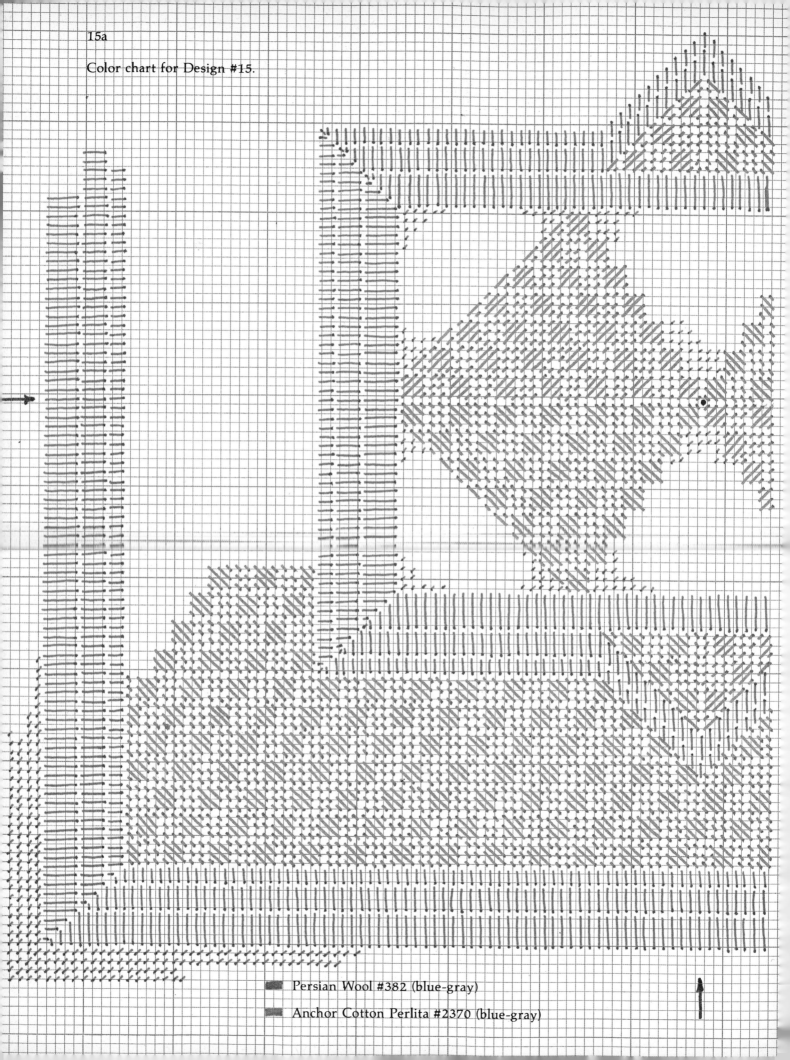

Persian Wool #382 (blue-gray)

Anchor Cotton Perlita #2370 (blue-gray)

Design 15

15b

Design #15. *Colonial Garden.*

Design #15. *Colonial Garden*
Pillow, 12″ × 14″, #10 canvas

Yarns:
Persian Wool #382 (blue-gray)
   Use full strand for all stitches
   Use 1 strand for continental-stitch allowance
Anchor Cotton Perlita #2370 (blue-gray)
   Use full strand for all stitches

On the chart the entire left half of the center motif is given but only somewhat more than one quarter of the total design is indicated by the black arrows pointing to the exact center dot. This center is in a canvas hole where 4 Scotch stitches meet. Cut your canvas to measure about 18 × 20 inches. Fold your taped canvas to find the approximate center and do these 4 Scotch stitches first with the perlita yarn.

Continue working out from the center and finish the arrow-like design in the center frame. Fill in the wool basketweave stitches and surround the area with the first frame of Gobelin stitches. Now, counting carefully, complete the triangular shaped motif that interrupts the framework. Finish the Gobelin stitch border from the center outward in rows of decreasing stitch lengths as shown (15A).

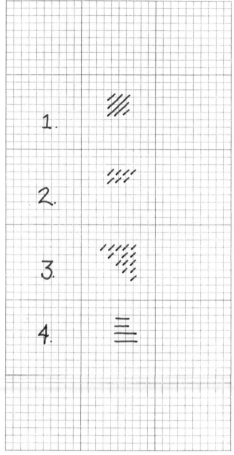

15c

Stitch key for Design #15.
1. Scotch
2. Continental
3. Basketweave
4. Gobelin

Begin sewing the background at the lower left corner of the last Gobelin stitch frame, as shown on the chart. The pattern will fall in place from this point. The Scotch stitches alternating with the continental stitches produce a slightly bias textural surface with the lovely sheen of the perlita yarn (15B).

The outer frames of Gobelin are in reverse order from those surrounding the center, growing larger as they near the outer edge. Finish your needlepoint with 4 rows of Continental stitch for a larger seam allowance to show off this border detail. Antique satin fabric was used as a backing (see color picture 11 in Chapter III).

Color chart for Design #16.

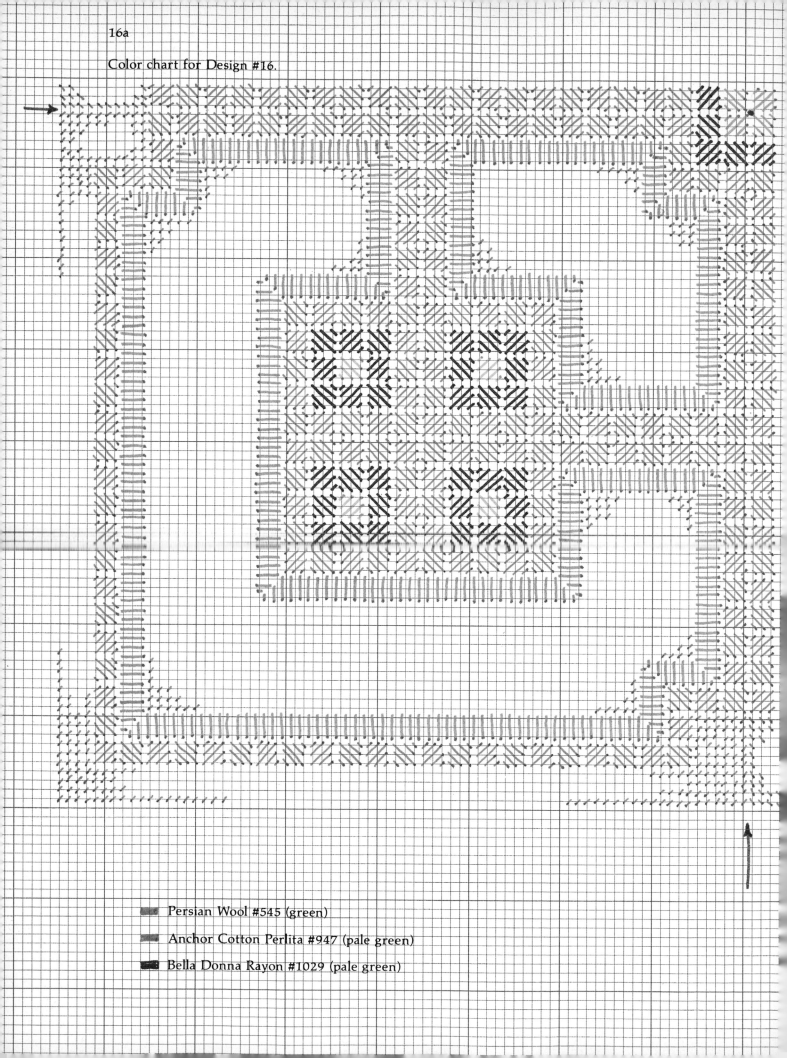

Persian Wool #545 (green)

Anchor Cotton Perlita #947 (pale green)

Bella Donna Rayon #1029 (pale green)

Design 16

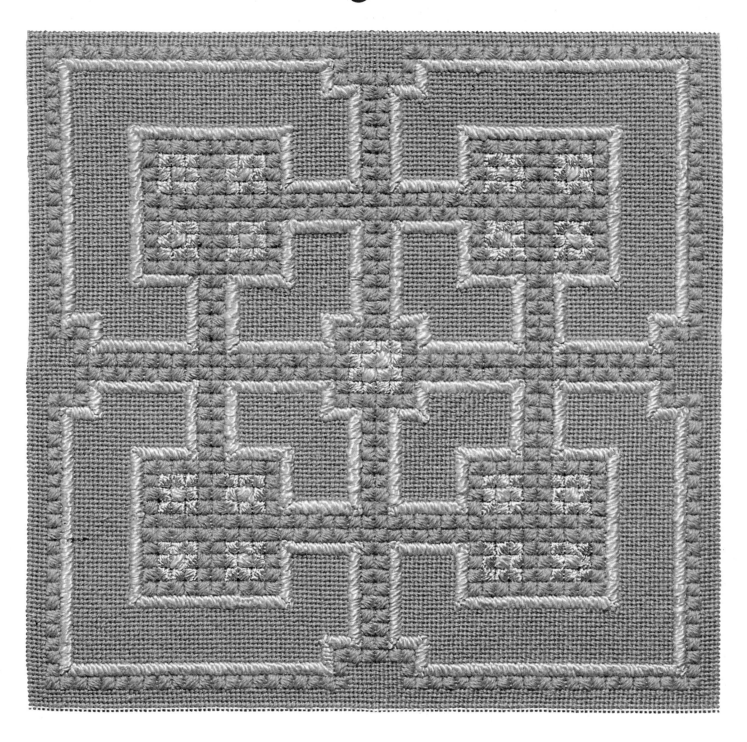

16b

Design #16. *Fern Forest.*

Design #16. *Fern Forest*
Pillow, 12" × 12", #12 canvas

Yarns:
Persian Wool #545 (green)
    Use full strand for Scotch stitches
    Use 2 strands for basketweave stitches
    Use 1 strand for Continental-stitch seam allowance
Anchor Cotton Perlita #947 (pale green)
    Use full strand
Bella Donna Rayon #1029 (pale green)
    Use double strand

With one quarter of the total design given in the chart, you can follow the black arrows to the center black dot. This dot, marking the exact center is in a canvas hole where 4 Scotch stitches meet. With your canvas cut to 18 × 18 inches, tape the edges and fold it into quarters to find the approximate center. Sew these 4 stitches first with the cotton perlita yarn. Work each additional row of Scotch stitches out from the center, changing yarns as indicated.

The only tricky thing about sewing this simple design is that I never watch the chart carefully enough and get carried away making too many Scotch stitches. So you are forewarned.

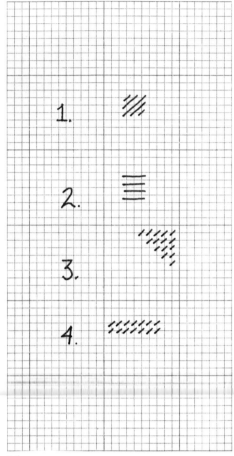

16c

Stitch key for Design #16.
1. Scotch
2. Gobelin
3. Basketweave
4. Continental

After completing the Gobelin stitch borders surrounding each Scotch stitch motif, do the basketweave background in the empty enclosed areas (16A). Because the chart shows only a quarter of the design, you will have to look closely at the photograph to see that the direction of the basketweave stitches changes in each quadrant. In other words, the stitches change direction in the center of each side, as shown near the black arrows on the chart (16A). Work each of the four sections of basketweave so that the stitches point toward the center.

Finish your design with 4 rows of continental stitch for a seam allowance adequate enough to show off that last border of Scotch stitches.

A linen fabric of soft green is used to back this pillow. Tassels, 3 1/2 inches long, are made up of all three yarns to attach at each corner for an added final touch (see color picture 10 in Chapter III).

17a

Color chart for Design #17.

Persian Wool #427 (gold)

Anchor Cotton Perlita #733 (light gold)

Anchor Cotton Perlita #798 (medium gold)

La Abuela Rayon Embroidery Perle #295 (gold)

Design 17

17b

Design #17. *Persian Braid.*

Design #17. *Persian Braid*
Pillow, 12" × 12", #10 canvas

Yarns:
Persian Wool #427 (gold)
　Use full strand for Gobelin stitches
　Use 2 strands for all other stitches
　Use 1 strand for continental-stitch seam allowance
Anchor Cotton Perlita #798 (medium gold)
Anchor Cotton Perlita #733 (light gold)
　Use full strand for all stitches
La Abuela Rayon Embroidery Perle #295 (gold)
　Use double strand for all stitches

For me, this design approaches the goal I set when this book began, to try to achieve the utmost with the materials given and the natural limitations of the craft. It combines interesting stitch arrangement with textured yarns and the close color values I like to work with. Your patience will be rewarded if you work this piece by counting with care, and just taking one step at a time. Try not to anticipate what you will be doing *next*, but concentrate on what you are doing *now*.

You have been given, in the chart, slightly more than one-quarter of the total design. The black arrows point to the exact center, which is marked with a black dot covering the point where 2 canvas threads cross. This intersection is covered by a cross-stitch of Persian wool. Fold your taped 18 × 18 inch canvas to find the approximate center and make this stitch first. Next do the 4 continental stitches in the same wool. Keep a close eye on the chart.

Change to the dark cotton perlita and sew the groups of 2 Gobelin stitches. With the wool, work the little cross-stitches that extend in lines out from the center to the edge of the center motif. Now, with the light perlita yarn, fill in the first group of variation cashmere stitches. Continue to work out from the center with the light perlita yarn, doing the next set of variation cashmere stitches.

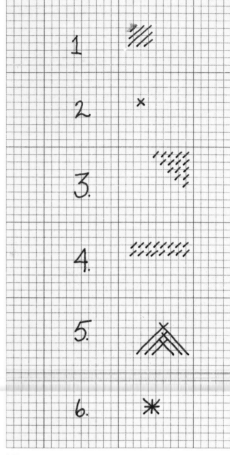

17c

Stitch key for Design #17.
1. Scotch
2. Cross-stitch
3. Basketweave
4. Continental
5. Rice
6. Smyrna Cross-stitch
7. Gobelin
8. Slanting Gobelin
9. A. Variation of Cashmere
9. B. Cashmere
10. A. Variation of Leaf
10. B. Leaf
11. A. Variation of Fern
11. B. Fern

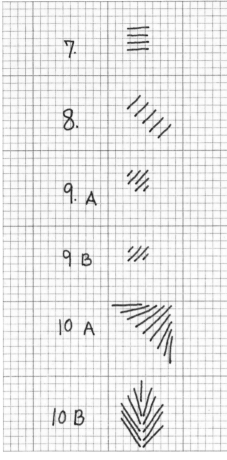

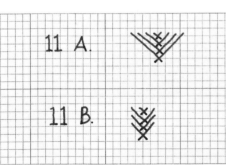

Continue in the same methodical step-by-step manner, referring to the chart and counting carefully. Work all the way around the center, sewing each stitch on the canvas precisely in its place. When you have completed the center motif, make the rows of little cross-stitches that divide the total design into quarters.

Now, relax, the hard part is done and you can enjoy doing the basketweave background. The only thing to watch is the change in stitch direction in each quarter, as shown on the chart near the lines of cross-stitches. The Gobelin stitch border uses both shades of perlita cotton to carry the texture and color out to the edge of the canvas. Finish your needlepoint with 4 rows of continental stitch to allow room for this interesting border to show.

Tassels, 3 1/2 inches long, are made up of both light and dark cotton yarns as well as the wool, and tied together with the rayon thread. And the pillow is backed with corduroy of a color matching the darkest cotton perlita to make a handsome finish (see color picture 12 in Chapter III).

18a

Color chart for Design #18.

Persian Wool #225 (rust)

DMC Mat Cotton #2919 (rust)

Zwicky Silk #2146 (rust)

Design 18

18b

Design #18. *Licorice Squares.*

Design #18. *Licorice Squares*
Glasses case, 3" × 6 1/2", #12 canvas

Yarns:
Persian Wool #225 (rust)
    Use full strand for eyelet stitches
    Use 2 strands for Scotch stitches
    Use 2 strands for continental stitches
    Use 1 strand for continental-stitch seam allowance
DMC Mat Cotton #2919 (rust)
    Use double strand
Zwicky Silk #2146 (rust)
    Use double strand

This repeat pattern is very easy to sew and works up quickly. I have used it in two ways, as a glasses case (18B) and a handbag. For the glasses case, the chart is by thread count, exactly the size you will sew it; that is, the chart represents front *and* back of the case. Directions for finishing the handbag, and an outline chart for the pattern are given in the demonstration section of Chapter III, along with instructions for assembling the glasses case.

Prepare your canvas, measuring 12 × 12 inches, by taping the edges and begin sewing with the wool. Sew the first eyelet stitch in one of the corners. Now, working one side of the glasses case at a time, do that row of 4 eyelet stitches. Changing yarns, as indicated on the chart, work the half Scotch stitches across the top. In the same manner, and changing yarns again, work the half Scotch stitches across the bottom. Repeat these two rows for the entire pattern. Work both sides of the case this way.

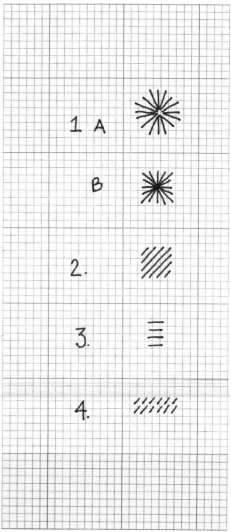

18c

Stitch key for Design #18.
1. A. Variation of the Eyelet
1. B. Eyelet
2. Scotch
3. Gobelin
4. Continental

Finish with the Gobelin borders and do that one last row of continental stitches down the center. When the case is folded along the center line this little row makes a nice beading around the edge. It is not necessary to use a seam allowance of needlepoint for a glasses case. However, since you do not make a *needlepoint* seam allowance, be sure to leave at least one half inch of unworked canvas seam allowance for sewing (see color picture 4 in Chapter III).

An attractive handbag can be created from the design shown here. Full instructions may be found beginning on page 125.

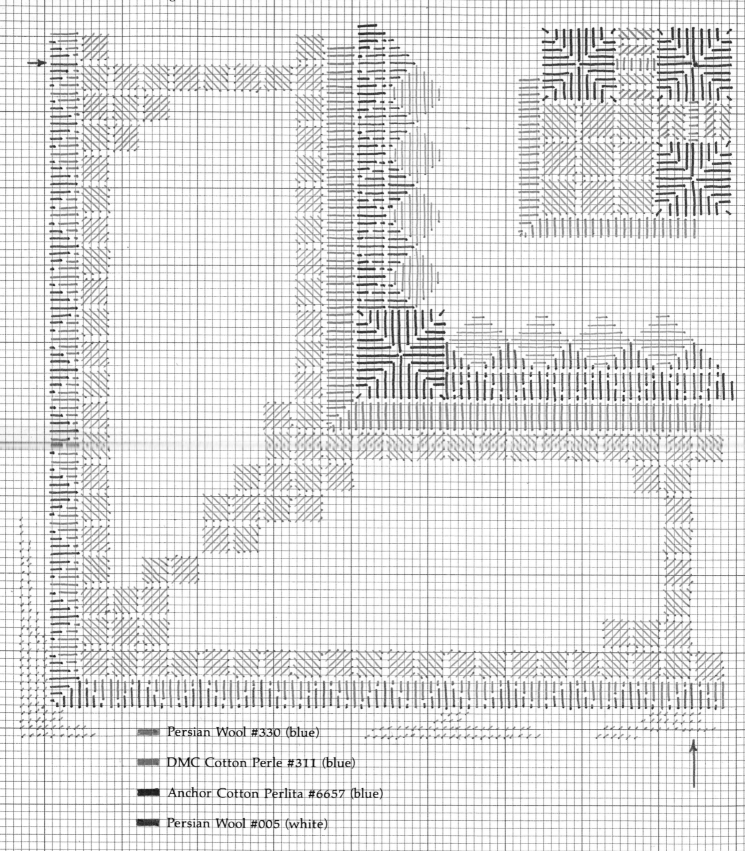

19a

Color chart for Design #19.

Persian Wool #330 (blue)

DMC Cotton Perle #311 (blue)

Anchor Cotton Perlita #6657 (blue)

Persian Wool #005 (white)

Design 19

19b

Design #19. *Centennial.*

Design #19. *Centennial*
Pillow, 14" × 14", #12 canvas

Yarns:
Persian Wool #330 (blue)
  Use full strand for Scotch stitches
  Use full strand for Gobelin stitches
  Use 2 strands for basketweave stitches
Persian Wool #005 (white)
  Use full strand for Gobelin stitches
  Use 1 strand for continental-stitch seam allowance
DMC Cotton Perle #311 (blue)
  Use triple strand
Anchor Cotton Perlita #6657 (blue)
  Use full strand

The chart gives you one quarter of the total design. Black arrows point to the black dot marking the exact center. This dot is covering a canvas hole that is the center of a triangle stitch sewn with perlita yarn. Prepare your 20 × 20 inch canvas by taping the edges and folding into quarters to find the approximate center. Make the center triangle stitch first.

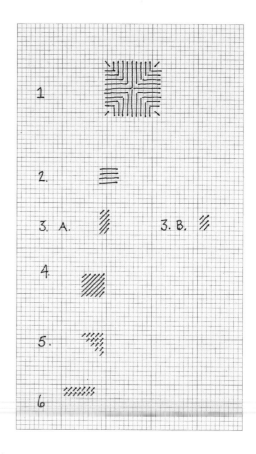

19c

Stitch key for Design #19.
1. Triangle
2. Gobelin
3. A. Extended Cashmere
3. B. Cashmere
4. Scotch
5. Basketweave
6. Continental

100

Working out from the center, change yarns as shown on the chart, and sew the rows of extended cashmere stitch next, and then the four small areas of Gobelin stitch that separate the extended cashmere stitches from one another. Make the 4 triangle stitches that surround the central triangle stitch. Fill in the wool Scotch stitches that finish the first square. Now, do the Gobelin border of cotton perle and surround this motif with basketweave stitches. These stitches are not drawn in the chart except for the small fill-in stitches at the corners of the central Gobelin border. Continue sewing in the same manner until the main square is completed.

Change to wool and carefully do the background of alternating Scotch stitches. Finish your pillow by repeating the detailed border of wool and cotton perle and adding 4 rows of continental stitch as a seam allowance.

This pillow is welted in white linen and backed with a matching blue fabric of ribbed antique satin (see color picture 17 in Chapter III).

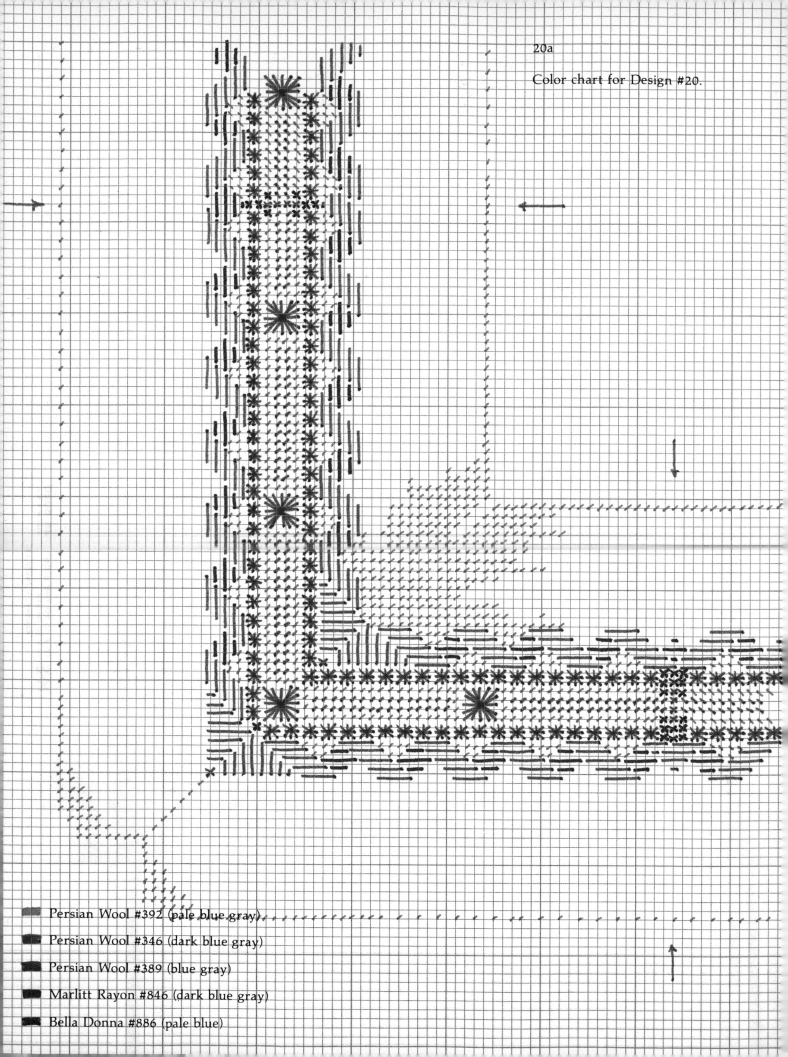

20a

Color chart for Design #20.

Persian Wool #392 (pale blue gray)

Persian Wool #346 (dark blue gray)

Persian Wool #389 (blue gray)

Marlitt Rayon #846 (dark blue gray)

Bella Donna #886 (pale blue)

Design 20

20b

Design #20. *Victorian Picture Frame.*

Design #20. *Victorian Picture Frame*

Frame, 11 3/4″ × 9 3/4″, for a 5″ × 7″ photograph, #12 canvas

Yarns:

Persian Wool #392 (pale blue gray)
  Use 2 strands for basketweave stitches
  Use 2 strands for continental stitches
Persian Wool #346 (dark blue gray)
  Use full strand for double leviathan stitches
  Use full strand for triangle stitches
  Use 2 strands for continental stitches
Persian Wool #389 (blue gray)
  Use 2 strands for Smyrna cross-stitches
  Use full strand for Gobelin stitches
Marlitt Rayon #846 (dark blue gray)
  Use double strand for cross-stitches
  Use double strand for Gobelin stitches
Bella Donna #886 (pale blue)
  Use double strand for cross-stitches

This romantic design is a favorite of mine. I hope you enjoy watching the motif develop as each yarn and each stitch take their proper place on the canvas. Count carefully and make sure the last, or top, threads of those Smyrna cross stitches and double leviathan stitches are consistent.

Prepare your 16 × 18-inch piece of canvas by taping the edges. The chart gives you slightly more than one quarter of the design, therefore only one of the four corners. The black arrows in this chart do not point to the geometric center of the canvas, which would be in the empty central space, but show the halfway point of each of the sides.

The easiest way to sew this needlepoint pattern is to begin in a corner, sew in both directions toward the adjacent corners and then close the rectangle by working to the last corner diagonally from where you began. In this way, by forming a correctly counted basic rectangle, you may proceed to embellish your work without concern, for accuracy will be assured.

About 4 1/2 inches into the canvas, on the bias, from the lower left corner, begin sewing with the corner triangle stitch. Changing yarns as indicated on the chart, work the 28 Smyrna cross-stitches up the side of the frame to the center motif at the halfway point, marked by black arrows on the chart.

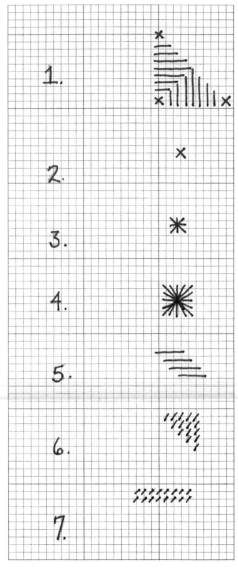

20c

Stitch key for Design #20.
1. Triangle
2. Cross-stitch
3. Smyrna Cross-stitch
4. Double Leviathan
5. Gobelin
6. Basketweave
7. Continental

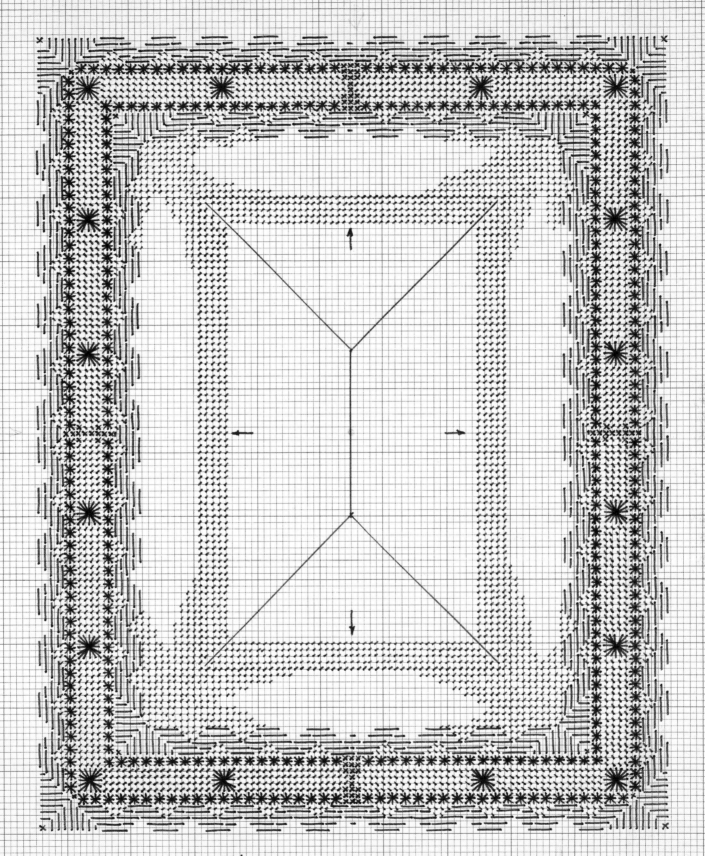

20d

Diagram showing stitching chart for Design #20 with unbroken lines indicating where the canvas must be cut so that it can be folded and glued around the wooden frame. Where these lines extend into the stitched area, a single row of stitches has been left unworked, as shown on the color chart for Design #20, page 102.

Then, go back to the corner and sew the 21 Smyrna cross-stitches across the bottom to the center motif at the halfway point, also marked with black arrows.

Return again to the lower left corner and, with the proper yarn, make the double leviathan stitches up the side to the center and across the bottom to the center. Now, fill in the continental stitch detail between the double leviathan stitches. Sew the inside row of Smyrna cross-stitches. This forms a ribbon-like the L-shape. At this point, I count those center stitches and canvas threads very carefully that make up the little fancy motif that decorates the frame at the center top and bottom and the center sides (20B). Leave these canvas threads bare, as we will return to them later. Continue sewing the continental stitches toward the other corners, putting the double leviathan stitches in their proper places. Sew the Smyrna cross-stitches into the corner and up to the right side, exactly the same way as you did the left side. Sew this ribbon shape all the way around the frame, creating the four-cornered outline of the piece.

Fill in the triangle stitches at each corner. Sew the rayon cross-stitches that were previously left out of each center motif. Now, do that tiny cross-stitch directly at the center of each of the corner triangle stitches.

Taking careful note of the way those Gobelin stitches change direction at the black arrows, make these stitches around the outside and the inside of your frame, using the wool indicated. Finish with the rayon yarn by sewing the rayon Gobelin stitches that join the wool Gobelin stitches all around the inside and the outside of the outline.

Using the main color of wool, finish your design with the basketweave background, doing the outside corners exactly as shown on the chart and *leaving* that bias row of canvas threads bare which points into each corner on the inside of your frame, as indicated by the empty graph lines on chart 20A. This is where you will cut to fold the needlepoint around the frame (see color picture 2 in Chapter III), as described more fully on page 113. You may want to do those last 4 inner rows in continental stitch, instead of basketweave stitch, sewing back and forth. These are shown in the black-and-white chart on which the empty bias rows are marked by a straight line, which indicates a cutting line (20 D).

The fully mounted needlepoint frame with a matted and mounted photograph of Mrs. Edmonds and her family. Full instructions may be found beginning on page 109.

III. PROJECTS AND DEMONSTRATIONS

The following pages should give you a good idea of how your needlepoint will look when it is made up into a finished project. There are color pictures of the pillows, cushions, frames, and cases made from the designs given in Chapter II.

Before the color section, we will continue with instructions for Design 20, with yarns and materials for making the yellow variation of the frame, so you will have a choice of colors. Of course, you can follow these instructions for the blue-gray frame just described. After the photographic demonstration of how to mount the frame and the proper way to mount a picture in this frame, there are complete instructions for making a glasses case and a handbag from the needlepoint in Design 18.

Directions for Making and Assembling the Yellow Victorian Picture Frame (Design 20)

Yarns:

Persian Wool #446 (blue on Chart 20A=yellow)
  Use 2 strands for basketweave stitches
  Use 2 strands for continental stitches

Suede Spun "Copper"* (orange on Chart 20A=orange)
  Use double strand for triangle stitches
  Use full strand for double leviathan stitches
  Use full strand for continental stitches

Persian Wool #005 (brown on Chart 20A=white)
  Use full strand for Gobelin stitches
  Use 2 strands for continental stitches

Pearsall Filo-Floss #156 (red on Chart 20A=orange)
  Use triple strand for cross-stitches
  Use triple strand for Gobelin stitches

Pearsall Twisted Silk #47 (purple on Chart 20A=yellow)
  Use triple strand for cross-stitches

*Also available in Spinnerin Yarn under the name *Baroque.*

Materials:

6 feet of Streamline Base Moulding, 3/8" × 2 7/16"
    Cut and miter 2 pieces:
        outside measurement: 11 7/16"
        inside measurement: 6 1/2"
    Cut and miter 2 pieces:
        outside measurement: 9 7/16"
        inside measurement: 4 1/2"
Upson Board, 3/16" thick, 9 7/16" × 11 7/16"
Mat Board, 4 ply, 9 7/16" × 11 7/16"
Non-glare glass, 1/16" thick, 5" × 7"
    (available at some hardware stores and at framing shops)
Your own photograph, 5" × 7"
1/2 yd. woven fabric (I used linen table napkins)
White household glue
Sheet of typing paper
An iron, set to medium-hot
4 decorative upholstery nails
12 nails, 19 gauge, 1/2" long
8 thumbtacks
Scissors, ruler, hammer, mat knife, and toothpick
Decorative brass easel
    (available in department stores, gift shops, etc.)

Color picture 1 in this chapter shows the yellow needle-point frame next to the blue-gray one already described in Chapter II. The same stitching pattern (20A) is used for both.

Matting and Mounting Demonstration

Assemble the moulding pieces into a frame and glue the corners together, as shown (A). Place your frame directly on top of the Upson Board and mark around the inside rectangle with a pencil (B).

A. Matting and mounting demonstration: the frame pieces, unassembled and assembled; the needlepoint, uncut and cut at the corners.

B. Matting and mounting demonstration: using the assembled frame to trace an outline on the Upson board.

Now you are ready to cover the frame with your needlepoint. Cut out the corners of your needlepoint canvas right up to the very *last row* of stitches (A, at right). Handle these corners carefully after cutting. Fold the needlepoint around the outside of the frame. Place a thumbtack at each side of all four outside corners, using two tacks to each side.

Remove the tacks on one side, leaving the others in place. Put glue on the edge of the wood frame and press the needlepoint, with your hands, firmly to the frame. With a piece of typing paper to protect the needlepoint, press this edge with a medium hot iron for several minutes until the glue is set as shown in C for the inside corners, which will be described later. Do the outside corners on the opposite side next, then the remaining two sides. Use your iron at each corner to help the stitches meet exactly right and to see that they are neatly joined. A toothpick will be useful to push in those inevitable stray stitches. Turn the frame over, trim the deep canvas overlap around the outside edges to about 1 inch and glue flat (C). Iron to set the glue.

Cut the center hole of your canvas up *to the stitches*, as indicated by the straight lines on the chart (20D), making deep Vs into the four inside canvas corners, which you have left unstitched. Working from the back, put some glue on one side of the wood frame and smear it around with a toothpick.

Pull the needlepoint canvas through the center of the frame as shown (C). Smooth with your fingers. Cover the needlepoint with paper and press firmly with the warm iron until the glue is set. Repeat for all four sides. Again trim the canvas and glue to the back of the wood frame. Press to set glue. Set your covered frame aside until ready to use in the mounting of the photograph.

C. Matting and mounting demonstration: mounting the needlepoint on the wooden frame.

You have already marked the center rectangle on the Upson board, using the wood frame as a guide (B). Now with your ruler, measure 5/16 inch into the frame from this penciled line and draw a second rectangle.

Place the pre-cut piece of glass on this rectangle to make certain it will fit into the area when it is cut out. If your glass is *larger* than the penciled lines, trace around the glass and use *this* line as your cutting line.

With the mat knife, carefully cut out the center rectangle as shown. Set the center cut-out aside until later.

Thin your glue slightly with water in a little dish. Spread the glue around the edges and on one side of the Upson board frame, about 1 inch from the edge, as shown at the right of (D). This photograph shows the three steps in cutting out the Upson board. (You will end with only one piece to cut out and cover.) Cover with fabric, and, with paper on top to protect it, press with a warm iron to set the glue. Cut away the excess fabric, as shown. Turn over and glue the back in the same way as the front. Set aside with the other pieces until ready to assemble.

D. Matting and mounting demonstration: three steps in cutting out the Upson board. The outline from the traced board (see step B) is cut, and the cut-out used to back the photograph. The frame is covered at the edges with cloth.

Cover one side of the mat board with fabric, using the thinned glue. Turn wrong side up and glue the edges in about 1 inch. Miter the corners of the fabric and smooth down. With paper to protect your fabric, press with a warm iron to set the glue. Again, the photograph (E) shows three stages in making the mat board. (You end with only one piece covered with fabric.)

Now assemble all your pieces (F). You have, beginning on the left: the fabric coverd mat-board backing, the Upson board with its fabric-covered edges, your glass covered photograph on top of the Upson board center cut-out, and the needlepoint-covered wood frame, shown face down.

Place the Upson board frame exactly square on the top of the face-down needlepoint frame (G). Hammer two nails on each side of the corners and one nail in the center of each of the four sides. Place the cleaned glass in the hole, then your photograph, which must also be face down, and last, the Upson board cutout.

Cover with the mat board, fabric-covered side out. Attach by nailing a decorative tack into each corner, as shown. For the finished frame, see color pictures 1 and 2 in this chapter.

E. Matting and mounting demonstration: three steps in covering the mat board with fabric.

F. Matting and mounting demonstration: all the assembled pieces.

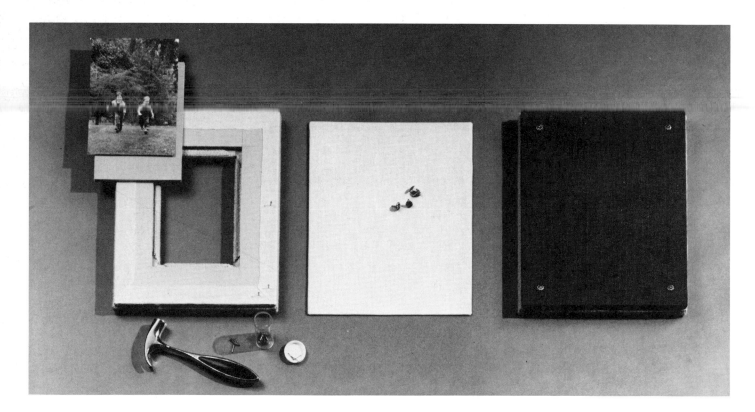

G. Matting and mounting demonstration: putting the frame together. The covered Upson board is nailed to the back of the needlepoint frame; the glass, photo and backing for photo set inside; and finally the mat board, with the fabric side out, is tacked in place. The center square shown here is not a functional part of the frame.

Directions for Assembling the Glasses Case (Design 18)

Try this method of lining glasses cases and sewing them together. First, trim the extra canvas around the outside edge to one half inch, and use this piece as your pattern for the lining. I use soft woven fabric of rayon or silk for linings, but I often use pillow cases or table napkins to get the color I need.

Join the lining to your needlepoint case along the top edge, with right sides together, by machine stitching. Turn to the right side, with seam allowance *underneath* the lining, and top stitch on the lining side a fraction below your machine stitching.

Now, fold in half lengthwise, with right sides together. Begin your machine stitching at the bottom of the needlepoint case at the fold. Sew across the bottom and straight up the side, the length of both the needlepoint and the lining.

After clipping seams and trimming, turn to the right side. Hand stitch the bottom of the lining to close. Tuck the lining into the case.

With a tiny back stitch, hand sew through both lining and needlepoint around the top of your case, about one-quarter inch from the edge, to give it a sharply creased appearance (see color picture 4).

Color pictures shown opposite:

1. Yellow variation of *Victorian Picture Frame*, Design #20, page 109.
2. *Victorian Picture Frame*, Design #20.
3. Handbag, variation of *Licorice Squares*, Design #18, page 125.
4. Glasses case, variation of *Licorice Squares*, Design #18.

5. Pillow, *Hop Scotches*, Design #10.
6. Pillow, *Coronet*, Design #11.
7. Pillow, *Sunflower*, Design #4.
8. Pillow, *Bittersweet*, Design #3.

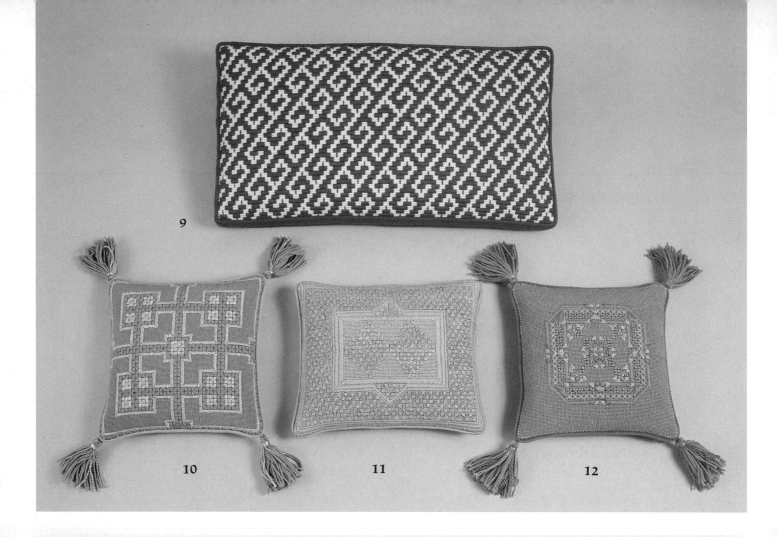

9

10 11 12

13

14

15

16

22. *Plaid for a Bamboo Chair*, Design #7.

Directions for Making the Handbag (Design 18)

#12 canvas (beige)

7" handbag frame, for a bag 7" deep × 8" wide

1 yard black cording for handle

2 feet of narrow gold cording (the kind used for gift wrapping, approximately 1/8" wide)

white household glue

Yarns:

Persian Wool #050 (blue on Chart 18A=black)

    Use full strand for eyelet stitches

    Use 2 strands for Scotch stitches

DMC Embroidery Floss #310 (green on Chart 18A=black)

    Use double strand

DMC Cotton Perle #310 (red on Chart 18A=black)

    Use double strand

Cut your canvas 16 × 20 inches and tape the edges. On a piece of paper trace the pattern, one half of which is given here (18D). The line of *dashes* indicates a *fold* which forms the bottom of the bag. Mark your canvas with a waterproof pen (see page 16) as indicated by the *solid* black line on the chart. Place the fold line in the center of the canvas and trace the whole pattern. The *dotted* line indicates a seam allowance, which we will ignore for the present.

Begin sewing your needlepoint pattern with the one eyelet stitch shown on the chart (18D), in the center of the fold line at the bottom. Cover the canvas, between your pen lines, with the pattern in the same way as described in the instructions for the glasses case (page 96), repeating row after row (see Charts 18A and 18C in Chapter II).

Since the dotted line indicates a seam allowance, remember that you do not sew needlepoint in this area, because it would make your seams much too thick. When your needlepoint is completely finished, cut your handbag *on the dotted line*. This will leave an unworked seam allowance of canvas as described. Using this piece as a pattern, cut out your lining fabric, and you are ready to assemble the handbag. Lining fabric of rayon or silk is available in yard goods stores.

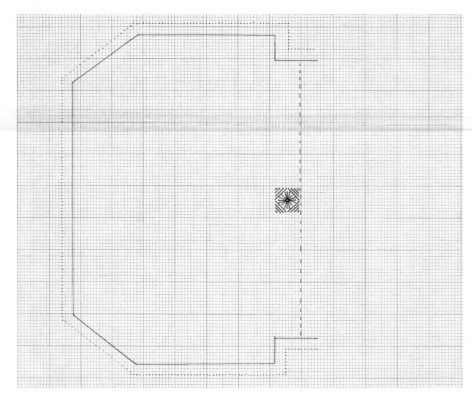

18d

Diagram showing outline for handbag. Note carefully that the dashed line indicates a fold, and the shape will be made again in mirror image on the other side of the fold. Also the areas outside of the unbroken lines, indicated by a line of dots, are to remain as unstitched seam allowance. The heavy lines on the chart paper represent 1 inch square in the pattern.

Directions for Assembling the Handbag (Design 18)

Sew the side seams of both the lining and the needlepoint separately, by machine, from the folded bottom up to the point where the sides slope in toward the center. Lock your stitching by back stitching or tying the threads.

Hand sew the needlepoint to the outside of the frame, through the holes, using a sturdy cotton carpet thread. Take tiny back stitches through to the outside of the needlepoint. With matching thread, they will not show. Needlepoint shops generally carry these frames, and some will mail them. Sometimes great finds can be had at antique shows and fairs for modest prices.

Tuck the lining inside the bag and hand sew it to the inside of the frame with little back stitches through the holes in the frame. To cover all of those hand stitches that show around the inside of your frame, glue the small gold cord right over the top of them.

I replaced the gold chain handle that came with my frame by a doubled black silk cording (see color picture 3 in this chapter.) After removing the chain, I threaded the cord through the brass loops on top of the frame. Using black embroidery floss, I bound the two handles together just above the loops, hiding the joined ends of the cord underneath.

SUPPLIERS

(Will fill mail orders)

The Knittery
2040 Union Street
San Francisco, Calif. 94123

The Needlewoman Shop
146 Regent Street
London S.W. 1 England

Eye of the Needle
Vintage 1870
Yountville, Calif. 94599

Needlepoint Blocking Device
Meyer Enterprises, Inc.
P.O. Box 644
Sharon, Pa. 16146

For fabrics and mounting:
Lee's Pillow Trunk
3924 Atlantic Avenue
Long Beach, Calif. 90807

REFERENCES

Caulfeild, S. F. A. and Saward, Blanche C. *The Dictionary of Needlework.* L. Upcott Gill, 1882. My use of the first edition was invaluable to me. It is now available from Crown Publishers, New York, 1972.

Hanley, Hope. *Needlepoint.* New York: Scribner's, 1964.

Ireys, Katherine. *Finishing and Mounting Your Needlepoint Pieces.* New York: Crowell, 1973. It is very important for a needlewoman to know how to finish needlepoint correctly. After so much hard work, it would be a shame to ruin it.

Sidney, Sylvia. *Sylvia Sidney Needlepoint Book.* New York: Van Nostrand Reinhold, 1968.

Snook, Barbara. *Needlework Stitches.* New York, Crown, 1963.

INDEX OF STITCHES

Numbers refer to the Designs in the book. Where variations
of stitches are referred to, the base stitch is also given on
the stitch key accompanying the indicated Design.